XVIII CENTURY SPANISH MUSIC
VILLANCICOS OF
JUAN FRANCÉS DE IRIBARREN

BY
MARTA SANCHEZ

LATIN AMERICAN LITERARY REVIEW PRESS
SERIES: EXPLORATIONS
PITTSBURGH, PENNSYLVANIA

Yvette E. Miller, Editor

1988

© Copyright 1988 by Marta Sánchez

Library of Congress Cataloging in Publication Data

Sánchez, Marta.
    Spanish Villancicos of the 18th Century

ML410.F818S26 1988 784.1'2 86-33800
ISBN 0-935480-26-9

Spanish Villancicos of the 18th Century can be ordered directly from the publisher, Latin American Literary Review Press, P.O. Box 8385, Pittsburgh, Pennsylvania 15218.

To my Sister   *To my Husband*

ACKNOWLEDGEMENT

It would have been impossible to complete this book without a great deal of help and cooperation. To the many people who contributed their time and knowledge my sincere gratitude.

As much of this research was done in Malaga, Spain, I would first like to express my acknowledgement to Don Justo Novo de Vega, vicar of the diocese of Malaga, for generously opening the doors of the Cathedral archives. My appreciation also to Father Andrés Llorden, O.S.A., for directing my attention to material pertinent to this study.

To Dr. Donald R. Beikman, Professor Colin C. Sterne and Professor Juan Adolfo Vazquez, I offer special thanks for their careful reading of the text and revising of the musical transcriptions. To Dr. Norris L. Stephens, my sincere appreciation for being always available for consultation and advice.

To Dr. Robert S. Lord, I would like to convey my deepest gratitude. His scholarly ability, his encouragement and understanding were vital to the completion of this book.

I am indebted to my friend and colleague Judith Heastings for her invaluable help with the transcription of the manuscripts; and to my friends Randy Kane and Roberta Weissberg, who gave many hours to read and discuss problems of the text.

Finally I would like to express my recognition to my sister for her constant encouragement and to my husband for his unlimited patience during the completion of this book.

TABLE OF CONTENTS

PART ONE

PART TWO

Music Transcriptions of Villancicos
by Juan Francés de Iribarren

CHAPTER I

The Villancico in the Eighteenth-Century Spain:
An Introduction

To the student of Spanish music, the eighteenth century unfolds a kaleidoscopic view of foreign musical influences and national assertions. The rule of the Bourbons, established in Spain in 1701, maintained musical links with France and officially supported Italian musicians. Spanish people, in turn, endorsed the reaffirmative nationalistic positions shared by the majority of their composers. Nevertheless, foreign baroque forms and compositional procedures permeated the musical output of native musicians, and these influences are reflected in many of their works. This coexistence of ultramontane and national tendencies was particularly successful in the *villancico*.[1]

The eighteenth-century villancico is a vocal composition in two or more movements with instrumental accompaniment. Its different movements include compositions unique to the traditional Spanish lyric as well as recitatives, arias, and baroque dance forms adapted to the vocal media. Cultivated primarily as a religious composition, the eighteenth-century villancico was widely performed on major religious feast days. The constant demand for new compositions accounts for the large number of villancicos preserved in libraries and archives of Spanish churches and monasteries.

One large source of villancicos of the eighteenth century is the Malaga Cathedral, an important music center since the sixteenth century. The Cathedral houses the work of Juan Francés de Iribarren, who served as Chapelmaster from 1733 to 1767, and was one of the most prolific composers among the Cathedral's chapelmasters.

The work of Juan Francés de Iribarren, and particularly his villancicos, has been singled out by the Spanish scholars Miguel Querol Gavaldá and Rafael Mitjana, among others, as perhaps the most genuine representation of Spanish religious music of the eighteenth century.[2] However, with the exception of a few of his compositions published in scholarly collections, the work of this composer has remained in manuscript form and is practically unknown.

The eighteenth-century villancico, a unique literary and musical manifestation of the Spanish people, has its roots in the primitive popular lyric of the Iberian Peninsula. In the mid-fifteenth century, the terms villancico, *villancete*, and *villancillo* began to be loosely applied to a great variety of songs. As used today, in reference to early forms, the term villancico identifies only the traditional strophic form which in

---

[1]   Villancico will not be italicized hereafter.

[2]   *Encyclopédie de la Musique et Dictionnaire du Conservatoire*, 1920 ed., s.v., "Espagne," by Rafael Mitjana. Iribarren's hymn, *Vexilla Regis*, is reproduced in this article as an example of eighteenth-century Spanish religious music. *Música Barroca Española* 5 (Barcelona: Consejo Superior de Investigaciones Científicas, 1973). Three Iribarren villancicos and one motet are transcribed in this volume.

the late fifteenth and early sixteenth centuries consisted of a short two-to-four line stanza, either used alone or followed by one or more glossing stanzas.

The villancico of this period attracted the attention of contemporary literary men and court composers, who showed their interest in this expression of the popular lyric by creating a new type of composition which had the traditional villancico as a point of departure. This learned villancico, called *cortés* or "courtly" villancico, retained the language and subject matter of the traditional form. However, the verse structure of the short initial stanza or *estribillo*, and of the glossing stanzas or *coplas*, was adapted to conform to the tendencies of erudite poetry.

The texts of these earlier villancicos were primarily secular, expressing love, humor, and the daily events of life. Very few were based on religious texts. But toward the end of the sixteenth century, composers of villancicos turned their attention more and more to liturgical subjects, and by the eighteenth century, the villancico prevailed almost exclusively as a composition with religious text.

The early villancicos were polyphonic compositions scored for two to five voices with or without instrumental accompaniment. During the sixteenth century, many villancicos were composed for soloists accompanied by lute or *vihuela de mano*.[3] Some of the more popular villancico melodies were subsequently used for instrumental variations. In the seventeenth century, the single movement structure of the villancico, influenced by Europe's more modern styles and by Spanish secular forms, began to be transformed into a multisectional composition with continuo and instrumental accompaniment. The villancico continued to develop along these same lines during the eighteenth century.

Interest in the religious villancico reached its peak in the eighteenth century. Its liturgical importance is emphasized by the fact that candidates for most chapelmaster positions were required to demonstrate an ability to compose in this genre. But with the passing of the baroque forms and declining interest in popular traditional compositions, which had been the intrinsic component movements of the eighteenth-century villancico, this unique religious manifestation of

---

[3] References to this string instrument date back to the twelfth century, with the first specific written reference found in the "Poema de Alfonso X" (1328). Well into the fifteenth century, the *vihuela* was played only with the fingers. Later in the century, two types of *vihuelas* appeared: the *vihuela de peñola*, played with a plectrum, and the *vihuela de arco*, played with a bow. The plectrum *vihuela* is a sort of hybrid of the guitar and the lute.

The *vihuela* and the guitar underwent modification during this time, becoming similar in shape and size, differing primarily in their respective number of strings. The *vihuela* occasionally had five strings, more often six or seven, the guitar had four strings, and toward the end of the century was found with five. Most important, the *vihuela* was played *punteado* (plucked); the guitar was strummed. From José Subirá, *Historia de la Música Española e Hispanoamericana* (Barcelona: Salvat Editories, S.A., 1953), pp. 204-6.

the lyricism and piety of the Spanish people gradually disappeared. By the first decade of the nineteenth century, performances of villancicos had been replaced in Spanish churches and monasteries by musical responsories. Today, compositions called villancicos are sung during the Christmas season in Spain and Hispano-America, but this designation has become synonymous with the Christmas carol.

The abundance of religious villancicos available from the seventeenth and eighteenth centuries in Spain demonstrates both the liturgical importance of the genre and the great amount of energy that Spanish composers directed to composition in this field. However, villancicos for the most part have remained in manuscript form, a fact which has contributed to the general unfamiliarity with the form itself and with the men who produced these compositions.

Iribarren was a composer of some reputation in his time, and some of his compositions were even performed in the Spanish colonies of the New World.[4] Nevertheless, he is almost unknown at present, despite his more than eight hundred extant manuscripts, over five hundred of which are villancicos. Iribarren's obscurity is a fate which has been shared by most of his contemporaries and peers.

In part, the minimization of Spain's musical patrimony from this period can be attributed to a lack of printed sources. Publishing of Spanish music during the seventeenth and eighteenth centuries was nearly non-existent.[5] This situation affected religious music more than secular, and was particularly true for the villancico, usually a "one-hearing" composition, which was not intended to circulate outside the church in which it was performed.

Before a comprehensive evaluation of eighteenth-century Spanish music can be made, the works of the composers of this period must be examined.[6] Because of the various types of compositions used in the villancico movements, an inclusive study of this form would shed light not only on the development of Spanish religious music but also on baroque and Spanish secular forms of expression.

---

[4] *Renaissance and Baroque Musical Sources in the Americas*, (Washington, D.C.: General Secretariat, Organization of American States, 1970), p. 10.

[5] During the sixteenth century and into the seventeenth century, native composers had opportunities to see their works published in cities such as Madrid, Barcelona, Valladolid, Valencia, Saragosse, and Alcalá. However, late in the seventeenth century and throughout the eighteenth century, predominant interest in French and Italian music brought close to a standstill the publication of Spanish music in Spain.

[6] For the last decades, musicological research in Spain has been sponsored by the Consejo Superior de Investigaciones Científicas and the Marsh Foundation. From this country, important contributions to the study of the music of Spain have been made by Gilbert Chase and Robert M. Stevenson. Specific research in the early villancico has been presented by Isabel Pope, who was a pioneer in this field; Padre Soler's villancicos have been examined by Sister Teresita Espinosa; Robert M. Stevenson has looked for villancico sources in Latin-America; and the Spaniard Vicente Ripollés has investigated the eighteenth-century villancico in Valencia.

In an attempt to contribute to a more accurate stylistic, formal, and aesthetic assessment of the villancico, the goals of this book are:

- To bring to light the villancicos of Juan Francés de Irribarren; to analyse formally and stylistically forty-seven of the villancicos available at the Malaga Cathedral; and to transcribe five of those selected.
- To introduce the composer and to provide a catalogue of all of his compositions as were available in 1973 when the author visited the Malaga Cathedral.
- To offer a historical survey of the Malaga Cathedral where Juan Francés de Iribarren worked for thirty-four years.

In choosing representative examples of Iribarren's villancicos, certain criteria were necessary. The selection, therefore, was based on the following:

- Dates of compositions.
- Occasions of performance.
- Instrumentation.
- Number of vocal parts.
- Use of learned and popular material.

This book expects to bring a better understanding of the villancico as a musical form, and particularly to those written by Juan Francés de Iribarren.

CHAPTER II

THE MALAGA CATHEDRAL: A HISTORICAL BACKGROUND OF THE EDIFICE, PERSONNEL AND VERNACULAR TRADITIONS

The Malaga Cathedral, where Iribarren spent his most productive years as a composer, was founded by Ferdinand of Aragon (1452-1516) and Isabella of Castile (1451-1504). It was built as a symbol of the return of Catholicism to the Spanish territories which had been under Moslem domination for almost seven centuries.[1] During his tenure there, Iribarren witnessed the efforts of the ecclesiastical chapter, or *Cabildo,* to complete the construction of the Cathedral.

The history of the Malaga Cathedral begins on 18 August 1487 with the surrender of the key to the city to Caballero Mosen Gutierre de Cardenas, Comendador Mayor de Leon, and representative of the crown[2]. Malaga, an active seaport and communication center, was one of the last of the Caliphs' strongholds to be recovered by the Christian armies. To celebrate their victory the armies displayed the banners of the monarchs and of the apostle St. James, and a cross was elevated on the highest tower of the Alcazaba [3] As an affirmation of the Christian faith, the prelates blessed the *Mesquita Mayor,* or principal mosque, and consecrated it as the city Cathedral.[4]

An account of the Cathedral's consecration by Boleas y Sintas, probably based on tradition, depicts Queen Isabella barefoot, humbly dressed, and weeping as she walked behind the Virgin's image. The Queen had donated the statue for this occasion, adorning it with her royal garments and jewels. After the image was placed in the Cathedral, the King and Queen attended a thanksgiving Mass, and a solemn *Te Deum laudamus* was sung as a religious benediction to their political victory.[5]

In another description of the consecration of the Mosque, J.M. Carriazo says:

---

[1]   The Malaga Cathedral belonged to the *Patronato Real.* In Spain, the Royal Patronage had been granted to patrons and founders of churches and religious foundations. In return for their financial support, the patrons could present for papal approval their own candidates for major and minor ecclesiastical benefices. In an effort to consolidate their political as well as their religious power, the Kings asked the Holy See to reaffirm their Royal Patronage privileges in Malaga, as they had for other territories in the Iberian Peninsula and the New World.

[2]   Miguel Boleas y Sintas, *La Catedral de Málaga,* (Malaga: Talleres de Imprenta de Arturo Gilabert, 1894), p. 119.

[3]   An Islamic palace-fortress.

[4]   *Ibid.,* p. 119.

[5]   *Ibid.,* pp 7-9.

...e las trompetas hicieron muy grande sonido, e los atabales e tamborinos, de tal manera que parecia todo el mundo estar alli. E los prelados y clericos e religiosos que alli se hallaron cantaron en alta voz el Te Duen laudamus...[6]

...and the sounds of the trumpets and the drums were so strong that it seemed as if the whole world were there. And the prelates, clerics and priests who were present sang the *Te Deum* laudamus...

Ferdinand and Isabella appointed Don Pedro de Toledo y Ovalle as the first bishop of the restored diocese of Malaga.[7] He assumed his office on 13 June 1488, almost a year after the reconquest of the city. Two days later he made public the statutes of his church and proceeded to designate personnel for the liturgical services and administrative functions of the diocese.[8]

The staff appointed by Toledo consisted of twenty canons, eight of them dignitaries of the church, and twenty chaplains insuring assistance and solemnity in the divine service. They were obliged to reside at the Cathedral, to celebrate Masses at some of the chapels, and to attend most of the religious services.[9] In subsequent years, three of the existing canonries were reassigned: one to a *Jurista* (1525), who served as an *ex officio* counselor of the Cathedral; one to a *Magistral de Pulpito* (c. 1536), a preacher who specialized in the Holy Scriptures; and one to a *Magistral de Escritura Electoral* (c. 1558), a teacher of the Holy Scriptures.[10] The chapelmastership was a beneficed position at the Malaga Cathedral. The first chapelmaster, Hernan (or Fernán) Lopez, was appointed in 1513.[11] This same administrative structure remained almost unchanged through the time that Juan Francés de Iribarren served there.

---

[6] *Crónica de los Reyes Católicos* (Madrid: 1927) p. 269.

[7] The first diocese of Malaga was probably created in the first century A.D. Following the Islamic invasion, the Visigothic Catholic organizations were left practically unchanged; but periods of persecution under Moslem rule, and sparse contact with the main trends of Christendom led to the weakening of Christian institutions. The diocese of Malaga seems to have ceased its activities at the end of the eleventh century, when many Mozarabs were forced to flee to North Africa.

[8] Boleas y Sintas, *La Catedral*, p. 7.

[9] *Ibid.*, pp. 7-9. The full staff of the Malaga Cathedral consisted of the deacon of Malaga, archdeacon of Malaga, archdeacon of Ronda, archdeacon of Velez, chantry, treasurer and succentor. In addition there were twelve priests, twelve acolytes, a minor sexton, an organist, a bell-toller, a verger, a beadle, a church-warden, a chapter notary, and two mayor-domos, one for the Church and the other for the Chapter.

[10] *Ibid.*, pp. 7-9.

[11] *Ibid.*, p. 13.

In February 1488, Gonzalez de Mendoza[12] granted permission for the erection of a permanent Cathedral, but insufficient funds delayed the construction.[13] The *Acta Capitular* of 29 March 1528 reports that Bernardino Contreras, on behalf of the Patriarch of Alexandria and Bishop of Malaga, addressed important Malagan citizens and members of the ecclesiastical and city *Cabildo*:

> ...con la ayuda de Nuestro Señor el queria hacer comenzar a edificar la iglesia Mayor de esta Cibdad, para lo cual el ha hecho una de muestra e traza e ha hecho venir a esta Cibdad al Maestro Enrique.[14] Maestro Mayor de La Iglesia de Toledo, asi para que viese dicha traza, como para que viese el lugar y sitio donde la dicha Iglesia se ha de edificar y sobre todo diese su parecer...[15]

> ...with the aid of the Lord, he would like to start the construction of the principal church of this city, for which purpose he had had a first draft made and had asked *Maestro* Enrique, superintendent of construction at the Toledo Cathedral, to come to evaluate where the church will be built...

In spite of the Contreras' efforts, construction was further delayed for twenty-one years. In January 1549, at the Cabildo's suggestion, Don Fray Bernardo Enrique, current bishop of Malaga, commissioned both Andres de Valdevira,[16] *Maestro Mayor* in Ubeda, and Diego de Vergara, *Maestro Mayor* of the Cathedral, to draft plans for the new church.[17] In June of the following year the *Maestros* presented their

---

[12] Gonzalez de Mendoza (1428-1495) was the son of the Marquis of Santillana. With his episcopal and familial influence he supported the ascension of Isabella to the Castilian throne. In return she retained him as Chancellor and Chief Advisor of Castile until his death. Known as the third king of Spain, he was a typical renaissance man. He patronized new learning; encouraged writers and scholars; and translated Homer, Ovid and Virgil into Spanish. He also wrote a catechism and in 1484 founded the College of Santa Cruz at Valladolid for students from the lower economic strata. *New Catholic Encyclopedia*, 1967 ed., s.v. "Mendoza, Gonzalez de," by D.W. Lomax.

[13] By 1500 the fund raising began on a small scale. Not until 1528 did Don Bernardino de Contreras, acting bishop of Malaga for Don Cesar Riario, take the first steps toward construction of the new church. Malaga Cathedral, *Acta Capitular*.
Note: Hereafter the *Actas Capitulares* of the Malaga Cathedral will be abbreviated *A.C.*

[14] Enrique de Egas, son of Hanequin de Egas, was responsible for important works in the cities of Jaén, Placensia, Granada, Seville and Santiago de Compostela.

[15] Boleas y Sintas, *La Catedral*, p. 146.

[16] Architect of the Jaén Cathedral. Influenced by the Gothic style, he designed the Cathedral as a single order of grouped shafts.

[17] *A.C.*, 6 January 1549. Cited in Boleas y Sintas, *La Catedral*, p. 153.

projects to the *Cabildo* and to Fernan Ruiz, who acted as a consultant.[18] It is not certain whose plans were accepted, but Vergara supervised work on the new construction.[19]

The seven chapels surrounding the main chapel of the new Cathedral were completed by 1564; the transepts in 1565; and the apse, main chapel, and crossing by 1587. The still unfinished Cathedral was inaugurated on 31 August 1588 by Don Garcia de Haro, bishop of the Malaga diocese. Construction of the *coro*[20] was started in 1592; and, although still unfinished, it was opened in 1632 for the use of the clergy. Construction then ceased for almost a century.

In July 1719, when the *Cabildo* ordered some roof repairs, the engineers' report stated that not only the roof but the entire building was deteriorating and needed basic reconditioning. Alarmed by this situation, the *Cabildo* decided that the Cathedral should be completed. A fund raising campaign was extended to all towns in the diocese, and contributions were solicited from both King Phillip V and the city. The *Cabildo* members each pledged 1000 *ducados* a year plus gifts in money and assets, in addition to relinquishing their rights of accretion.[21]

The *Cabildo* engaged the services of José Bada to resume construction of the Cathedral. The first cornerstone was laid on 21 May 1721. Discrepancies in architectural and ornamental styles between the earlier and later construction support the assumption that the original plans used by Diego de Vergara were lost. To start the construction José Bada had to adapt some of the existing drawings, which are attributed to a *Maestro Ayala*.[22] After Bada's[23] death, the building was continued by Antonio Ramos, who had been working under Bada since 1723. The work slowed down in subsequent years, either from lack of confidence in the new *Maestro Mayor* or because of financial problems.

In 1764 Juan Francés de Iribarren witnessed the linking of the old with the new construction. The north tower was finished in 1769; but in 1782, while the south tower was under construction, King Charles III ordered the *Cabildo* to suspend all work on the Cathedral. The order seems to have been triggered by alleged administrative abuses of the construction budget by the *Cabildo*.[24] Repeated efforts to change the

---

[18] *A.C.,* 20 June 1550. Cited in Boleas y Sintas, *La Catedral*, p. 154.

[19] In the interim the Mesquita Mayor, known today as the *Iglesia Vieja* or Old Church, was used as the Cathedral.

[20] The *coro* of the Spanish cathedrals is a separate structure blocking the central nave.

[21] *Ibid.,* pp. 170-71.

[22] *Ibid.,* pp. 176-90.

[23] Died in Granada around 1756.

[24] *Ibid.,* p. 328. Construction expenses for the older part of the building were 1,115,417.00 *reales* and 16,000 *maravedies*. From 1719 to 1782, expenses rose to 12,304,000.00 *reales*, an exorbitant amount then even if the devaluation of Spanish currency is taken into consideration. Of this amount 9,777,896.00 *reales* were provided by the Spanish crown. The remainder of the budget was covered by the *Cabildo* members.

King's mind were unsuccessful, and later attempts to resume the work under succeeding governments failed.

The still unfinished Cathedral of Malaga is one of the largest churches of Spain. The building measures 375 feet in length, 240 feet in width, and 130 feet in height. It is located in the center of the city of Malaga, surrounded by beautiful, well-kept gardens. Impressive white marble steps lead to the main entrances facing the *Plaza del Obispo*. The original plans called for two massive towers, each 280 feet high, to flank the north and south sides of the main structure. The incomplete south tower, 224 feet high, has become known as the *Torre Mocha* (Cropped Tower).

The interior of the Cathedral consists of a central nave separated from the two side naves by eight pillars. The Church contains fifteen chapels and twenty-five altars. The main altar, designed by Jose Frapoli, is made of white and black marble. Light filters through ninety windows and thirty large skylights, illuminating the beautiful white marble and serpentine stone used in the floors, columns, and interior ornamentation.

The *coro bajo*, used by clerics and benefices, has 103 stalls in Renaissance style which have been attributed to Alonso Cano in collaboration with Michel and Pedro de Mena. The two large organs,[25] which stand on both sides and above the *coro*, were built in 1781-82 by Don Julian de la Orden, master organ builder of Cuenca Cathedral, who was commissioned by the Malaga *Cabildo* in 1778.[26] The organ cases were designed by Don José Martin Aldehuela, an architect of Malaga.[27]

The most renowned Spanish artists and craftsmen worked at the Malaga Cathedral, including Pedro de Mena, Alonso Cano, Cerezo and Morales. Their works are considered the most valuable treasures of the Cathedral. Unfortunately, through political upheavals many of the artistic riches of the building have disappeared.

The recreation of the diocese of Malaga in the late fifteenth century brought about the reunification of the people of Andalucia with the main body of the Spanish Church. In accordance with Church statutes, the newly founded cathedral had the same privileges and obligations to the crown and to the Pope as those of other Spanish churches. The Cathedral adopted a similar administrative organization and proceeded with the liturgical usage of the time. Most important to the study of the historical background of the villancico in the Malaga

---

[25] The organ used in Iribarren's time was built in 1660 by Claudio Osorio, *maestro organero* of Seville. From P. Andres Llorden, "Notas de los maestros organeros que trabajaron en Malaga." *Anuario Musical*, 43, (1958): 174-77.

[26] Boleas y Sintas, *La Catedral*, p. 238.

[27] For a description of the organs' construction, see: Joseph A. Burns, "Malaga Cathedral Organs are Fine Specimen." *The Diapason* (November, 1960): 8-9. Both organs were preserved through the Spanish Civil War of the nineteen-thirties. One of them, however, lost many metal pipes which were sold as scrap. The other one is in perhaps the best state of preservation and repair of any Baroque organ in Spain. Both instruments are practically identical and have been provided with modern electric blowers, without any other change as to wind pressure or tracker action.

Cathedral was the incorporation of traditional theatrical and musical performances in the vernacular to some church festivities.

Church rituals popular at the time of the founding of the Malaga Cathedral included the singing of *burlas* and *chanzonetas*, the performance of Christmas and Corpus Christi plays, and the farce of the *Obispillo* (boy-bishop). Presented on Innocent's Day and St. Nicholas' Day, the farce entailed a choirboy taking the place of the bishop, dressing in the episcopal clothes, and conducting the entire day's ceremony with the assistance of the rest of the choirboys. The bishop and prebendaries, in turn, assumed the role of the boys, and treated the latter with the utmost respect and obedience. The last record of the performance of the *Obispillo* is dated 2 December 1543. It was terminated by petition to the members of the *Cabildo*, as the ceremony lent itself to abuses against the hierarchy of the Church. However, the symbolic tradition of the farce of the *Obispillo* was perpetuated. During Corpus Christi and St. Nicholas' Day festivities, a choirboy would conduct the singing at the chorister's desk, sing the psalms, and perform the Mass.[28]

Liturgical dramas had fallen into disuse by the time of the Malaga Cathedral's foundation, yet two theatrical presentations continued. One was for the feast of Corpus Christi; the other, for Christmas. The latter representation took place on Christmas Eve, intending to entertain the faithful and to ensure their attendance to the divine office.

The representation for Corpus Christi probably began in 1498, the year of the establishment of the Blessed Sacrament procession. The play was performed several times during the day; first, in front of the Blessed Sacrament in the Church, and then at predetermined stations of the procession throughout the city. It was conducted by the chapelmaster with the participation of the choirboys. In 1562, staging of the Corpus Christi play was removed to one of the Cathedral chapels, due to increasing irreverence toward Church matters. By 1577, the plays were barred completely from inside the church, and were tolerated only at some of the porticoes. However, the plays continued to be performed during the procession.[29]

A prevalent practice in Spanish churches and monasteries had been the singing of compositions in the vernacular during the most solemn Church festivities. Songs called *chanzonetas* and *burlas* began to be performed at the Malaga Cathedral in the sixteenth century.

Chanzonetas and *burlas* were light and festive songs usually sung at Christmas, Epiphany, Blessed Sacrament, and Immaculate

---

[28] Boleas y Sintas, *La Catedral*, pp. 22-28.
[29] *Ibid.*, pp. 29-30.

Conception Day.[30] The purpose of *chanzonetas* and *burlas*, as later that of the villancico, was twofold: to entertain the congregation and to clarify the meaning of a particular celebration. However, as a result of the popular character of these songs, texts were often infiltrated by satiric and facetious remarks detrimental to religious feasts and to the Church. To stop the abusive use of *chanzonetas*, and particularly of the derisive *burlas*, the Malaga Cathedral followed the policy adopted by other churches. Chapelmasters were released from regular church duties one month before an important liturgical event. During this period their responsibilities were to find appropriate texts for the songs, to write the music, and to have the compositions ready for the *Cabildo*'s approval fifteen days before the public performance. Despite the Church censorship, *chanzonetas* and *burlas* texts became more and more difficult to control. As a result, the singing of *burlas* at the Cathedral was suppressed in 1585[31] and *chanzonetas* were phased out of all liturgical services of churches and monasteries by the mid-seventeenth century.

During the seventeenth century, the fresh, unspoiled and fashionable villancico emerged as a welcome alternative to the *chanzonetas*. No references have been found indicating specific dates either for the exclusion of *chanzonetas* from the liturgical service or for the first performance of villancicos at the Malaga Cathedral. Records evince, however, that *chanzonetas* were still sung during the Christmas celebration of 1645. In the absence of Chapelmaster Juan Perez Roldán, whose resignation became effective in February of 1646, the senior prebendary Francisco Mangas was responsible for the preparation of the compositions.[32] With the examinations for the selection of a new chapelmaster scheduled for 2 October 1646, the *Cabildo* probably waited to entrust the new appointee to make the necessary changes in the musical policies of the Cathedral.

By the middle of the seventeenth century, the singing of villancicos was a common practice in most Spanish churches and monasteries. At the Malaga Cathedral, this practice was introduced—as far as it can be inferred from the information available in the *Actas Capitulares*—during the first chapelmastership of Francisco Ruiz de Samaniego (1647-54 and 1661-66). Two entries in the *Actas Capitulares* reinforce the assumption that villancicos were sung under the direction of Ruiz de Samaniego. One reveals that, before departing for Burgos,[33] Ruiz de Samaniego offered to leave the villancicos which he had

---

[30] The first reference to a performance of *chanzonetas* at the Malaga Cathedral is found in the *A.C.*, num. 10, fol. 23v., dated 16 October 1555. But Father A. Llordén, in "Notas históricas del personal de la Catedral de Malaga," *Anuario Musical* 16 (1961): 120, maintains that the performance of these songs began at an earlier date. Boleas y Sintas in *La Catedral*, p. 30., also implies an earlier date.

[31] *A.C.*, 7 June 1585.

[32] *A.C.*, num. 23, fol. 228.

[33] Ruiz de Samaniego was chapelmaster at the Burgos Cathedral from 1654 until 1661.

composed for the Christmas season.[34] The other entry, related to the forthcoming examinations to choose a replacement for Ruiz de Samaniego, lists the composition of a villancico as one of the important requirements to obtain the position of chapelmaster.[35]

Documentation about the villancicos available in the Cathedral archives is scarce. Nevertheless, some historical data related to the preparation of these compositions have been found. One reference discloses that Chapelmaster Alonso Torres (1666-83) was released from some of his church obligations one month before Christmas and Corpus Christi festivities in order to compose the villancicos for such occasions.[36] Another source attests that the *Cabildo* reminded Chapelmaster Francisco Sanz (1684-1732) that villancico texts needed diocesan approval "to ensure that decent things were sung."[37]

Chapelmasters always had difficulties in obtaining new and appropriate texts for the various church festivities. During the seventeenth and eighteenth centuries very few religious institutions had poets-in-residence in charge of writing original texts for each particular celebration. Even though, as Juan Francisco de Sayas asserted, compositions in the vernacular were easily understood and could serve as a meaningful vehicle of communication between the Church and the congregation.[38]

Juan Francés de Iribarren, who recognized the importance of using texts of literary quality which would be suitable for each occasion, petitioned the *Cabildo* in 1735 to appoint the poet José Guerra to write all of the texts for villancicos to be performed at the Cathedral.[39] He argued that it was a discredit to the Cathedral and humiliating for him to have to beg for new texts each year. He maintained that texts usually used in compositions performed during Immaculate Conception Day, Blessed Sacrament, Christmas, and Epiphany had already been sung at other churches.[40]

The singing of villancicos continued at the Malaga Cathedral until 1798; that is, during most of the tenure of Chapelmaster Jaime Torrens (1770-1803). However, the tradition of presenting new compositions at each important liturgical feast may have ceased in 1792. The *Acta Capitular* of November of that year reveals that Torrens, who had been ailing for some time, requested to be released from his obligations to compose villancicos for the oncoming Immaculate Conception Day and Christmas season. In consideration of his ill health, the *Cabildo* acceded

---

[34] *A.C.*, num. 26, fol. 355.

[35] *A.C.*, num. 26, fol. 363v.

[36] *A.C.*, num. 10, fol. 23v.

[37] *A.C.*, num. 39, fol. 158.

[38] *Música canónica, motética y sagrada, su origen y pureza con que la erigió Dios para sus alabanzas divinas* ...(Pamplona: José de Rada, c. 1761). Cited by Francisco José León Tello, *Teoría Española de la Música en los siglos* XVII y XVIII. (Madrid: Consejo Superior de Investigaciones Científicas, 1974).

[39] *A.C.*, num. 44, n. fol.

[40] *Ibid.*

to his request and authorized him to use the villancicos available in the Cathedral for those occasions.[41] Apparently Torrens was in delicate health for several years. Therefore, further investigation is needed to establish if new villancicos, written either by Torrens or by other composers, were performed at the Malaga Cathedral between the years 1792 and 1798.

By the end of the eighteenth century, the singing of villancicos had fallen into disuse in most Spanish churches and monasteries. The Malaga Cathedral was probably one of the few important churches to perpetuate the villancico tradition until the end of the century. The official revision of the musical policies in force at the Cathedral was brought about by a letter from Javier García, Chapelmaster at the Saragosse Cathedral. In his letter, read at the *Cabildo* meeting of 7 September 1798, García offered to send some of his musical responsories to be performed during the Christmas season. In support of his offer, the Chapelmaster pointed out that in all of the most reputable musical centers of Spain, responsories were sung in place of villancicos.[42]

García's statement was corroborated by the deacon, who also disclosed that in regard to the music for religious services, the deaconry had made certain decisions without consulting the *Cabildo*. According to the deacon's report, the diocese had already received a set of responsories from the chapelmaster of Salamanca Cathedral and commissioned others for the feasts of Immaculate Conception Day and Epiphany.[43]

The issue of retaining or excluding villancicos from the liturgical service was put to the vote. The *Cabildo* members, confronted with the musical policies of other churches and the deacon's endorsement of those policies, voted to exclude villancicos from all celebrations of the liturgical calendar.[44] The *Cabildo*'s decision brought to an end a 150-year tradition of villancico singing at the Malaga Cathedral.

[41] A.C., num 56, fol. 363.
[42] A.C, num. 57, fols. 519v. 520, 521v. 52, 536, 543v and 546.
[43] *Ibid.*
[44] *Ibid.*

CHAPTER III

A BIOGRAPHY OF JUAN FRANCÉS DE IRIBARREN

The position of chapelmaster at the Malaga Cathedral, a desirable and demanding appointment, had been held by some of the leading musicians of Spain.[1] The main duties of the office were to compose, plan, and conduct the music for the liturgical services, and to teach music to the choirboys.[2] Juan Francés de Iribarren conscientiously served Malaga in his years as chapelmaster, bringing innovations to the church and leaving a rich musical legacy preserved in the Cathedral's archives.

The procedures for filling the position of chapelmaster were governed by the rules of the Royal Patronage system, to which the Malaga Cathedral belonged. The first step required the chapter to gain permission from the *Real Consejo de la Cámara* for public distribution of edicts announcing the vacancy and inviting qualified musicians to compete for the post. After selecting a candidate, the *Cabildo* sent the appointment with the nominee's credentials to the king (*nombramiento*). The king, in turn, obtained a royal decree (*presentación*) from the *Real Consejo de la Cámara* asking the prelate of the diocese and the Cabildo to confer the prebend or benefice upon the candidate (*colación*).

To qualify for the position of chapelmaster, the candidate had to submit to a thorough musical examination which lasted many days.[3] Although there is scant information on the particular exams that Iribarren took, records of proceedings used in hiring his successor might elucidate the requirements of the Malaga Cathedral for that period. Chapelmaster candidates had to apply for the position within sixty days of the posting of the edicts, at the end of which time the examination took place. Arriving applicants stayed in the nearby convent of San Felipe Neri. The chapelmasters from the churches of Jaén and Seville were selected as judges with a per diem fee of sixty *reales* and an allowance of 1500 *reales* for travel and living expenses. The judged allowed the applicants thirty-four hours to compose a

---

[1] The most famous was Cristobal de Morales, chapelmaster from 1551 until his death in 1553. See: Appendix A.

[2] *A.C.*, num. 38, fol 83v. The *A.C.* of 2 June 1702 records that the *Cabildo* reminded the chapelmaster Francisco Sanz of his obligation to teach polyphony to the choirboys and to those members of the church who were willing to learn.

[3] From "Oposiciones al Magisterio de Capilla en España durante el Siglo XVIII," *Anuario Musical* 2 (1947): 195. José Artero describes a typical eighteenth-century examination in which the candidate had to compose: (1) a four-to-eight-part antiphon with a given *cantus firmus* that included eighty measures for the word Amen; (2) a motet that used all the structural techniques of canons, fugues, theme and development; and (3) an academic exercise in strict counterpoint. Most important of all, however, was the candidate's composition of a villancico with the following specifications: (1) a four-part introduction; (2) an eight-part *estribillo* with orchestra; (3) a recitativo with an instrumental or a thorough bass accompaniment; and (4) a solo aria.

villancico, instead of the customary twenty-four hours established in the edicts. After a day of rest, the applicants were given twenty-four hours to compose two or three verses of a psalm. On the following day the final exam took place in the *coro* of the Malaga Cathedral in the presence of the judges and members of the Church and the *Cabildo*. The applicants were given one half-hour to perform the works which they had brought with them, to be followed by the performance of their villancico and psalm. In addition to composing and performing their music, the examinees had to demonstrate ability in conducting and a theoretical knowledge of music.[4]

The position of chapelmaster at the Malaga Cathedral became vacant with the death of Francisco Sanz on 28 January 1732.[5] As the news of Sanz' death spread, applications for the post began to reach the *Cabildo* before an official announcement of the vacancy could be made. Juan Francés de Iribarren's application, dated 24 March 1732, was one of the earliest. Others were Manuel Martinez Delgado, organist at the Real Descalzas of Madrid; Miguel Malanco, professor of music, organist, and composer; and Juan Manuel de la Puente, chapelmaster at the city of Jaén. These four applications were received between 1 March and 9 June 1732.[6]

In the meeting on 18 April 1732, the *Cabildo* members pointed out that for such a prestigious position, undoubtedly there would be more applications than those already received in the few months since Sanz' death. Advertising and holding competitive exams to fill the vacancy were costly operations. The *Cabildo* was responsible for most of the applicants' expenses, which greatly increased the cost of the undertaking. The *Cabildo* was also aware that some musicians serving at important churches refused to acknowledge the edicts, thinking it beneath their professional dignity to apply for a job which was publicized. In light of these circumstances, and since the edicts had been dispensed with on previous occasions, the *Cabildo*, endorsed by the bishop, requested from the *Cámara Real* the omission of the edict procedure. As an alternative it was suggested that the candidates be selected on the basis of skill, musicianship, and reputation. On 12 September 1732, the *Cámara Real* granted the *Cabildo* permission to propose candidates for the position without publicizing the vacancy.[7]

There are no records of the final number of applications for the position, nor is there mention of the customary competitive examination. The only information available is that some of the applicants' works were performed on 17 October and 23 October 1732.[8]

After scrutinizing the applicants' backgrounds, the *Cabildo* selected two candidates for the position. Their first choice was Martinez Delgado; Juan Francés de Iribarren was their second choice. Martinez Delgado received official confirmation of his appointment on 14 March

---

4   A.C., num. 50, fols, 667v, 670, 671, 674v and 380.
5   The Sagrario Parish archives, *Obituary Book* (1636-1738), fol. 156.
6   A.C., num. 44, n. fol.
7   *Ibid.*
8   *Ibid.*

1733. A later record reports his death on 7 June 1733, implying that at the time of his appointment he was already in poor health:

> ...pues además de no haber dejado dineros algunos quedaba empeñado con el doctor Antonio Lozano, prebendado de esta iglesia, su albacea testamentario, en la cantidad de 200 ducados, siendo causa de estos gastos el continuo padecer tres meses fuera de su casa.[9]

> ...in addition to not leaving any money, he was indebted to Dr. Antonio Lozano, prebendary of this church and executor of his will, as a result of expenses incurred by three months of continuous illness and absence from home.

Soon afterwards the *Cabildo* must have offered the job to Iribarren, because the royal decree granting his appointment is dated 20 July 1733. He could assume his duties in Malaga in October of 1733, only after his genealogy and character references had been confirmed by the Church Council in Sanguesa, his birthplace.[10]

Juan Francés de Iribarren, son of Juan Francés de Iribarren and Agueda Chabarría, was born in 1698.[11] According to the *Diccionario de la Música Labor*, he served as organist in Salamanca until 10 May 1733, after which he became chapelmaster at an unidentified church in Granada from 10 October 1733 until 1737.[12] However, according to the *Acta Capitular* of 1 October 1733, Iribarren was already at Malaga, presenting the *Cabildo* with proof of his appointment, both of which were necessary in order to procure the position of chapelmaster.[13]

Moving to Malaga proved to be beyond Iribarren's means. The *Acta Capitular* of 14 October 1733 reports that the bishop and the *Cabildo* consented to his petition for financial aid to cover the costs of relocation. On 12 April 1734, still pleading economic difficulties, Iribarren presented another request to the *Cabildo* for a salary advance.[14]

One of Iribarren's early problems as chapelmaster was the difficulty of obtaining original texts needed to compose the villancicos. In all Spanish churches at that time, one of the primary and most demanding duties of the chapelmaster was the composing of villancicos for church festivities and religious occasions. In the *Acta Capitular* of 1 February 1735, there is a memorandum from Iribarren stating that he had to beg for new texts or borrow them from compositions that had already been performed in other churches, thus diminishing the reputation of the chapel by the lack of original texts. He proposed that José Guerra, poet of the King's chapel, be asked to write the necessary

---

9 *A.C.*, num. 44, n. fol.
10 *Ibid.*
11 *Ibid.* The writer lacks information about the day and month of his birth.
12 1954 ed., s.v. "Francés de Iribarren."
13 *A.C.*, num. 44, n. fol.
14 *Ibid.*

texts for the church festivities. The *Cabildo* accepted his proposal and allotted Guerra an annual salary of twenty-four *ducados* (ducats).[15]

Iribarren maintained a varied musical repertory for the liturgy. When he assumed his position, the Cathedral music archive was practically non-existent, either from lack of money or from negligence on the part of the individuals previously responsible for the liturgical music. In the *Cabildo* session of 8 February 1737, it is recorded that:

> ...si en dicho archivo no tuviese la iglesia misas, salmos motetes, salves, lamentaciones, misereres, villancicos, etc., porque no habrán de traer los músicos al coro las músicas bajas y envejecidas que han andado rodando por los conventos y parroquias de la ciudad, o con la muerte de un maestro de capilla han de enmudecer todos los músicos de vuestra señoria.[16]

> ...if Masses, motets, psalms, salves, Lamentations, Misereres, and villancicos, etc., were not available in such archives then the chorus would have to perform compositions of low quality and those that had been played over and over again in convents and parishes of the city, or with the death of a chapelmaster there would not be music available for the musicians to sing.

In order to solve this problem, the *Cabildo* in 1737 authorized two of its members to create a music library. With Iribarren's cooperation, they organized the available music and planned to provide a sufficient and worthwhile repertory. To augment the resources of the archives, Iribarren donated not only the compositions which he had written while in the service of the Cathedral, but also his works composed before coming to Malaga. He also recomended to the *Cabildo* that copies of his new works, as well as the works of his successors, be deposited in the archives.[17]

After eight years at Malaga, Iribarren notified the *Cabildo* that he had accepted the position of chapelmaster in Valladolid. In his letter of resignation read at the *Cabildo* meeting on 26 January 1741, he explained that his mother's health was poor and she was very lonely because he and his brother lived in Malaga, which was some distance from her home. The *Cabildo* members, who were appreciative of his abilities as chapelmaster, asked him to reconsider his decision and raised his salary by one hundred ducats a year with the understanding that, in the event of his death while in the service of the Church, this amount would be transferred to his mother for life.[18] Apparently this arrangement was acceptable to Iribarren because there are no further references to his leaving at this time.

---

[15] *A.C.*, num. 44, n. fol.
[16] *Ibid.*
[17] *A.C.*, num. 45, fol. 193.
[18] *Ibid.*

In spite of his increasing infirmity, Iribarren's responsibilities were compounded in his later years. The *Acta Capitular* of 27 November 1761 names Francisco Piera as temporary teacher of the *seises*.[19] On 7 February 1763 Piera claiming disciplinary problems, asked that he be released from his teaching obligatios and that the *Cabildo* take one hundred ducats of his salary to pay another teacher. His petition was denied.[20] On 7 February 1763 Piera again requested to be excused from his duties with the *seises* and this time the *Cabildo* agreed. The teaching reverted to Iribarren with an increase in salary of 100 ducats and the stipulation that, in deference to "his sufferings and weakness of the legs and head," he could continue to use the "lower" chair to conduct the music.[21]

Iribarren carried on his duties for three more years, but a crippling illness forced him to reconsider resignation in favor of living in retirement with his brother, who was a presbyter at the St. Augustine monastery in Malaga. In a letter to the *Cabildo* dated 8 April 1766, he expressed concern that his advanced age and the continuous and painful accidents caused by his illness were affecting the execution of his obligations as chapelmaster. He wrote that he wished to resign so that a competent person could carry on in his place. He proposed for himself a less demanding appointment within the diocese with an annual salary of four hundred ducats plus two *cahices* of wheat (the equivalent of thirty-seven bushels).[22]

The *Cabildo*, cognizant and grateful for Iribarren's thirty-threc years of service rendered to the Cathedral, was influenced to aid the ailing man in the last years of his life. The salary proposed by Iribarren was considered insufficient to cover his expenses, and unfair in view of his dedication to the church. On 2 May 1766, therefore, the *Cabildo* decided that he would retain his chapelmaster position at a full salary, and in addition to free medical care, he would be released from all official obligations.[23]

Iribarren's health declined rapidly. The Cathedral records of 2 September 1767 state that the chapelmaster died that day at 3:00 p.m. The funeral took place the next day following Malaga tradition. In accordance with his wishes, Iribarren was buried in the Cathedral.[24] He owned two houses which he bequeathed to his only brother, with the clause attached that, upon his brother's death, one of the properties would be transferred to the Cathedral and the other to the Augustinian

---

[19] *Seises* were children who participated with songs and dances in some church services and festivities. The term refers to the fact that there was usually a group of six boys usually under ten years of age.

[20] *A.C.*, num. 49, fol. 322.

[21] *A.C.*, num. 49, fols. 515r and 515v.

[22] *A.C.*, num. 50, fol. 250v.

[23] *A.C.*, num. 50, fols. 255v., 256r., and 256v.

[24] *A.C.*, num. 50 fol. 488v. Sagrario Parish Archives, *Obituary Book*, fol. 140 (1738-94).

convent. His savings were bequeathed to charity, and all his compositions were donated to the music archives of the Malaga Cathedral.[25]

---

[25] *A.C.*, num. 50 fol. 488v. Sagrario Parish Archives, *Obituary Book*, fol. 140 (1738-94). Notary of Juan Lopez Quartero, *Protocol Archives*, file 2471, fols. 493-98, 14 April 1763.

CHAPTER IV

COMPOSITIONS BY JUAN FRANCÉS DE IRIBARREN AVAILABLE AT THE MALAGA CATHEDRAL

Juan Francés de Iribarren was thirty-five years old when he assumed in 1733 the chapelmaster position at the Malaga Cathedral. During his thirty-four years of service to the Cathedral, he composed an enormous amount of religious music. In 1737 he donated 119 of his earlier works[1] to the newly organized music archives, and presumably he continued to add the scores of all of his new compositions. After Iribarren's death, in appreciation of the honors conferred upon the composer, his brother presented the *Cabildo* with a chest containing several of Iribarren's original manuscripts.[2] Theoretically then, the originals and copies of all Iribarren's compositions should be available in the Cathedral's music archives. Research into the archives has shown, however, that many of his works are missing.

Iribarren's compositions, which are housed in the Music Library of the Cathedral, are all in manuscript and are catalogued into forty-one *legajos*, or files. Legajos 1 to 20 contain 380 compositions consecutively numbered throughout. Within the remaining twenty-one *legajos*, which are not sequentially numbered, the compositions themselves are consecutively numbered, beginning with number one in each *legajo*.[3] In 1973, when the author visited the Cathedral, the number of available manuscripts, including original compositions and copies, was 894. For some works both the full scores and the parts were available; for others only the full scores or the parts could be found.

Iribarren's manuscripts have been preserved in very good condition. Their size is either 31 by 21-1/2 or obl. fol. 21-1/2 by 31 cms. The numbered leaves are all carefully hand-stitched. On the cover page, if there is one, and on the top of the first sheet of music itself, there is information concerning the name of the piece, the type of composition, the year, and the occasion on which it was performed.

Most of Iribarren's manuscripts have two different unrelated numbers indicating that the music material has been inventoried at least twice. One of the numbers corresponds to the actual organization of the manuscripts into *legajos*,[4] while the other denotes the position assigned to each composition catalogued in an inventory taken in 1770. There is evidence of another inventory in 1856, but it seems to have been

---

[1] P. Andrés Llordén, O.S.A., "Notas históricas de los maestros de capilla en la Catedral de Málaga (1641-1799)." *Anuario Musical* 20 (1967): 132.

[2] A.C., num. 50 fol. 490.

[3] See Appendix B for content of *legajos*. The compositions available at the Cathedral are tied in bundles. Each bundle contains approximately the number and type of compositions indicated in the corresponding *legajo*.

[4] Miguel Querol Gavaldá, in *Musica Barroca*, p. 10, refers to the cataloguing of Iribarren's manuscripts in *legajos*.

limited only to the cataloguing of printed music available in the archives.

The earliest known catalogue of the music in the Malaga Cathedral is the *Inventario Musical de 1770*, discovered by Father Andres Llorden.[5] This catalogue was jointly compiled by the canon Don Francisco Santos de San Pedro and Don Jaime Torrens,[6] Iribarren's successor. Most of the compositions listed belong to Iribarren. Other works included are by Jaime Torrens and by some of Iribarren's predecessors, Esteban Brito, Francisco Sanz, and Manuel Martinez Delgado. Compositions by Miguel Conejos (d. 1737), a former organist of the Cathedral, are also listed, as are compositions by representative Spanish composers who had not served at the Cathedral.[7]

The Iribarren compositions listed in the 1770 catalogue are organized into two large homogeneous groups: "Works with Latin Texts" and "Works in the Vernacular." In addition there are two smaller groups consisting of "Unbound Works with Latin Texts" and "Compositions Included in a Choir Book." The 273 compositions listed as "Works with Latin Texts" have been subdivided into Masses, Misereres, Lamentations, sequences, Vespers, *Te Deum Laudamus, Vexilla Regis, Pange Lingua,* Office of the Dead, Invitatories, *Salve Reginas, Regina Caeli,* Litanies, and motets. Within each of these subdivisions, the works have been broken down further into compositions with instruments and compositions without instruments. The consecutive numbering of the compositions within each group refers almost without exception to original scores, with no indication of the availability of duplicate scores. All entries are undated, and the incipits of the compositions are not given. The information supplied is restricted to the number of voice parts and the choice of instrument. If more than one instrument is to be used, the additional instruments are not specified. For motets, additional information is given concerning the religious function for which the music was performed.

Together the two smaller miscellaneous groups, "Unbound Works with Latin Texts" and "Compositions Included in a Choir Book,"

---

5 This catalogue was published by Father A. Llordén as "Inventario Musical de 1770 en la Catedral de Málaga" in *Anuario Musical* 24 (1970): 237-46.

6 *A.C.*, num. 51, fol. 243v. Torrens served as chapelmaster from 1770 until his death in 1803. He worked on this inventory during the first year of his appointment in Malaga. In a memorial addressed to the *Cabildo* he emphasized the state of maltreatment and dispersal in which he had found the musical patrimony of the Cathedral. Through his efforts most of the missing manuscripts were recovered, including more than 280 original works.

7 These composers are Tomás de Peñalosa, Fernando Fernandiere, Sebastian Aguilera, José de Torres, Prenestina, and Matías Ruiz. A copy of the 1770 inventory with new entries is dated 1771. The additions belong to the composers Pedro Rabassa, Maestro Galán, Maestro Contreras, José de San Juan, and Francisco Guerrero, who was appointed chapelmaster to the Malaga Cathedral in 1554 but resigned before taking possession of his job. The book of Masses, psalms, and Magnificats by Guerrero, catalogued in the 1771 inventory copy, was a gift from the composer to the Malaga *Cabildo*.

comprise a listing of compositions with Latin texts that includes psalms, motets, antiphons, Lamentations, *Magnificats, Nunc Dimitis, Benedicamus, Kyries, Sanctus, Agnus,* and *Te Deums.* All of these items are undated, and the number of voice parts is given only for the unbound compositions. In "Compositions Included in a Choir Book," only the numbers of the folios corresponding to each composition have been provided. In this latter grouping the first composition is listed as starting on folio 18. The absence of folios 1-17 suggests that either these folios were missing, or they did not contain music and, therefore, were not germane to the inventory.[8]

In the remaining large group, "Works in the Vernacular," Iribarren's works are organized under the subheading: "Christmas Villancicos," "Immaculate Conception Villancicos," and "Works for the Blessed Sacrament." After each entry in the catalogue, there is an indication of the availability of both the original scores and duplicates. Compositions are listed as "complete" if both originals and copies are available, and a notation is made if any are missing.[9] Only Christmas and Immaculate Conception villancicos are listed by years. The fact that the number of villancicos performed on these occasions is not specified implies that a fixed number of compositions was used every year.

To this effect, Dr. Robert Stevenson mentions that sets of nine villancicos, or eight villancicos closing with a *Te Deum,* became fashionable in the seventeenth century.[10] Villancicos were generally sung at matins. This canonical hour involves an invitatory and three divisions called nocturns. Each nocturn consists of three psalms with antiphons followed by three lessons, each of which is followed by a responsory. A different villancico was performed after each of the nine responsories, and sometimes a *Te Deum* replaced the last villancico.

The Christmas villancicos still available for the years 1733 through 1760 and the numerical indication found in the manuscripts, with reference to the order in which the compositions were to be performed, corroborates Stevenson's statement. Therefore, it can be concluded that the tradition at the Malaga Cathedral was to sing eight or nine villancicos for Christmas Day and one villancico for the Feast of Epiphany.[11] A tally of works composed by Iribarren from 1733 to 1760 should come to approximately 280. At the Music Library, however, there are at present only 255 compositions corresponding to those years.

For the feast of the Immaculate Conception, three villancicos seem to have been the rule.[12] Boleas y Sintas presents the texts of the three villancicos which were sung on the Immaculate Conception Day

---

[8] The choir book was not available for checking at the time of this research at the Malaga Cathedral.

[9] In accordance with Iribarren's suggestion for the music archives, every work seems to have been recopied from the original.

[10] *Renaissance and Barogue Musical Sources in the Americas,* (Washington, D.C.: General Secretariat, Organization of American States, 1970), pp. 9-11.

[11] See Catalogue of Iribarren's work in Appendix D.

[12] *Ibid.*

in 1734.[13] Again, if three villancicos were performed at this particular feast, Iribarren may have composed at least eighty-four compositions for the twenty-eight years listed in the 1770 catalogue; yet there are only sixty-four extant Iribarren compositions for this period.

Those compositions with texts in the vernacular which fall under the subheading of "Works for the Blessed Sacrament" are grouped into sixty-five arias, twenty-nine duets, seventy-two villancicos, and twenty-three villancicos listed as *Calendas*.[14] Of this number twenty-eight arias, four duets, 142 villancicos[15] and nineteen *Calendas* are actually deposited in the Music Library of the Cathedral. While it is possible that a small set of villancicos was sung at Matins and others during the procession of Corpus Christi, the fact that villancicos are not listed by years indicates that the number performed for the Blessed Sacrament feast could have varied from year to year.

Very few of Iribarren's compositions available at the Cathedral archives are undated or dated prior to 1733. It is difficult to ascertain what happened to the works which Iribarren composed before coming to Malaga or to the works which he donated to the Church when he became chapelmaster. One explanation is that earlier compostions were reused in Malaga and updated according to the year of performance. It is also possible that during the confusion of the Spanish Civil War (1936-39), some of the manuscripts were lost or destroyed, although the archives were considered to be relatively secure. It is also conceivable that further research, not limited to the Malaga Cathedral, will uncover other works either in Salamanca, where Iribarren held his previous position, or elsewhere.

The findings of two scholars are important indications that Iribarren's work was indeed known outside Spain. Dr. Robert Stevenson has reported the availability of several of Iribarren manuscripts in the archives of the Cathedral of Guatemala City in Guatemala.[16] Without mentioning the type of compositions, Miguel Querol Gavaldá states that there are ten works by Iribarren in the Cathedral archives of Las Palmas de Gran Canaria.[17]

According to footnotes of the "1770 Music Inventory," Christmas and Immaculate Conception villancicos of the years 1761 and 1762

---

[13] Boleas y Sintas, *La Catedral*, p. 44. There are no Immaculate Conception villancicos available for the years 1747, 1751 through 1754, and 1756.

[14] The "villancico de *Calenda*" seems to have been the first or opening villancico of a set. Iribarren wrote villancicos de *Calenda* for Christmas, the Blessed Sacrament, and Immaculate Conception Day.

[15] The number of Blessed Sacrament villancicos found in the archives is greater than those listed in the 1770 catalogue but there are many duplications.

[16] *Renaissance and Baroque Musical Sources,* p. 10. The following villancicos, which are also available at the Malaga Cathedral, are listed with some dates of performance at the Guatemala Cathedral: "De amor la oficina," "Marinero," "Que le diremos (1780)," "Digo que no he de cantarla (1764)," "Es el poder del hombre," "Vaya de Jácara (1764 and 1771)." The aria "Vesubio Soberano" and other items performed in 1775, 1786 and 1802 are also listed.

[17] Miguel Querol Gavaldá, *Música Barroca*, p. 10.

were missing as early as 1770. Starting with the year 1763, the inventory lists Christmas and Immaculate Conception Day works composed by Jaime Torrens and Martinez Delgado. In addition to the Iribarren works cited for the years 1733 to 1760, the inventory enters several of his scores composed before 1733 and about twenty from 1763 to 1766. Although these later works appeared to have been composed by Iribarren, some changes in style and musical calligraphy cast doubt concerning the identity of the composer. Hoping to facilitate further studies of Iribarren's work, a catalogue of his compositions available at the Malaga Cathedral has been prepared and is presented in Appendix D.

The existing wealth of Iribarren's musical works reveals that the diocese of Malaga has tried to preserve the Cathedral's musical patrimony. Iribarren's music, however, has not been heard for two hundred years and is practically unknown. His compositions, as well as those of other composers who worked at the Cathedral, have yet to be brought to light.

CHAPTER V

HISTORICAL BACKGROUND OF THE VILLANCICO

During the middle of the fifteenth century, some brief and simple poems began to appear in Spanish *cancioneros*.[1] These anonymous two-to-four-line poems, or *cancioncillas*, were later known as villancicos. Sometimes used as refrains for more extended poems, the *cancioncillas* were expressions of a popular and traditional lyricism far removed in language and style from the courtly poetry of the time. The earliest *cancioncillas* found in *cancioneros* are part of the song, "Por una gentil floresta." The song tells of a poet who, while hidden in the forest, listened to three lovelorn maidens singing popular refrains of folk tradition:

> Aguardan a mí
> Nunca tales guardas ví
>
> La ninya que los amores ha
> como dormira sola?
>
> Dexaldo al villano y pene
> vengar m'ha Dios delle

Realizing that he will never be loved by the maidens, the poet sadly intones:

> Sospirando va la ninya
> e non por mí
> que yo bien so lo entendí[2]

This anonymous song was included in later anthologies. In the *Cancionero Musical de Palacio*,[3] it is attributed to Suero de Ribera and presented as "Otro dezir de Suero de Ribera."[4] In two sixteenth-century publications, the *Pliego suelto de Praga* and the *Espejo de enamorados*, the same song is ascribed to Iñigo Lopez de Mendoza, Marquis of Santillana (1398-1458), and presented as "villancico, fecho por el marqués de Santillana a unas tres hijas suyas."[5]

---

[1] The *cancioneros* are collections of popular and courtly poetry and songs. They were compiled during the Middle Ages and Renaissance by poets, musicians and aristocrats.

[2] Antonio Sanchez Romeralo, *El Villancico* (Madrid: Editorial Gredos, S.A., 1969), p. 14.

[3] This *cancionero* is the most illustrative document of the musical trends of the Spanish court from approximately 1460 to 1504.

[4] "Another saying of Suero de Ribera." Sanchez Romeralo, *Villancico*, p. 35.

[5] "Villancico composed by the Marquis of Santillana for his three daughters". *Ibid.*, p. 14.

Sanchez Romeralo and other modern scholars think it unlikely that the writer of the song was either Suero de Ribera or Santillana. Sanchez Romeralo says that even if Santillana had written the song it is not likely he would have labeled it a villancico. He points out that in Santillana's *Prohemio al condestable de Portugal*, dated between 1445 and 1449, there is no mention of the term villancico, although the author discussed many poetic forms and techniques. Any use of the word villancico in Santillana's time, adds Sanchez Romeralo, would only connote poetry in a folk style, or poetry of the common people,[6] not a literary and musical form.[7]

Other early uses of similar terms can be found in two fifteenth-century collections. One anonymous composition labeled *villancillo* is included in the *Cancionero de Herberay des Essarts*, dated between 1461 and 1464. The poem consists of an introductory stanza of two lines and five stanzas of four lines each. The second line of the initial stanza is repeated as a refrain on the fourth line of each succeeding stanza.

> La niña gritillos dar
> non es de maravillar
>
> Mucho grita la cuitada
> con la voz desmesurada
> por se ver asaltada
> non es de maravillar.[8]

The *Cancionero de Stuñiga*, compiled around 1460, includes a composition by Carvajales[9] under the heading of *villancete*. The poem consists of one initial stanza of four lines and three stanzas of octosyllabic verses with consonant rhyme. The last two lines of the initial stanza are also repeated as a refrain at the end of each succeeding stanza. The initial stanzas of both poems[10] are in the popular vein, but the language, unlike that of the traditional *cancioncillas*, is cultivated and only imitative of the popular lyricism.[11]

The terms villancico, *villancillo* and *villancete* seem to have still been a novelty at the time the *Cancionero de Herberay des Essarts* and

---

6   The etymology of the word villancico has been traced to a diminutive form of the word *villano*, which in the Middle Ages denoted a serf or an individual of humble origin. This meaning supports the premise that the term villancico was originally coined to describe songs of popular tradition which were composed and sung by the folk *(villanos)*.

7   Sanchez Romeralo, *Villancico*, pp. 34-75.

8   Number 37 in the *Cancionero*.

9   Carvajales spent most of his life at the court of Alfonso V of Aragon.

10 The first composition is similar to a *zejel*, a poetic structure with refrain taken from the Arabic popular lyric. The second one can be described as a sophisticated *seranilla*, a lyric compositon similar to the troubadour *pastourelle*.

11 Sanchez Romeralo, *Villancico*, pp. 36-37.

the *Cancionero de Stuñiga* were compiled. Compositions with verse structure similar to those described above are, in both *cancioneros*, identified with other poetic forms. One authentic old cancionilla is even presented in the *Cancionero de Herberay des Essarts* as a *desfecha*[12] and not as a villancico. The term villancico came into wide use, however, at the end of the fifteenth century.

In the *cancioneros* of the British Museum (late fifteenth century), *General de Hernando del Castillo* (1511) and *Musical de Palacio*,[13] the term villancico was applied to a variety of songs with courtly themes and language as well as to the traditional *cancioncillas*. In these compilations, the villancico appeared either in the brief form of those *cancioncillas* attributed to Santillana or as an initial stanza followed by glossing stanzas of popular or courtly character. The term villancico is assigned to both structural types in the *Cancionero Musical de Palacio*, which contains the largest number of traditional *cancioncillas* (about sixty-six). In the *Cancionero de Juan del Encina* (1496), the term is reserved exclusively for the initial *cancioncilla*, and the appended stanzas are identified as *glosas, pies* or *vueltas*,—terms borrowed from learned poetry.

The origin and history of the *cancioncillas* is still a matter of speculation. The perfect simplicity of their style cannot be identified with any of the Spanish literary trends of the mid-fifteenth century or with the poetry of previous centuries. It can only be assumed that they are very old and that their style was shaped by an oral tradition which flourished apart from the mainstream of learned poetry.

Ramón Menendez Pidal postulated in 1919[14] that the *cancioncillas* belonged to a tradition that developed during the Middle Ages. His theory was based on certain thematic, formal, and expressive similarities between the villancico with glossing stanzas and the *cantigas de amigos* of Galician-Portuguese tradition.[15] The most important link between these poetic genres is the use of *paralelismo* and *encadenamiento* techniques,[16] which were practically unknown to the learned poets of the fifteenth century.

---

[12] Composition number 10 in the *Cancionero*. The *desfecha*, or *deshecha* is a short composition used as an interpolation or to end a longer poem with which it had a subject matter relation.

[13] It is necessary to point out that the classification of the compositions in this *Cancionero* comes from an index added to the *Cancionero* in the sixteenth century. This index registers 389 villancicos, 14 *estrambotes* (similar to the Italian frottole), 44 *romances* and 29 villancicos *Omnium Sanctorum*. The loss of 54 folios has reduced to 458 the number of compositions preserved.

[14] Conference given at the Ateneo of Madrid. Cited in Sanchez Romeralo, *Villancico*, p. 345.

[15] A fundamental source of study for these songs is the *Cantigas de Santa María*, collected and perhaps partly composed by Alfonso X of Castile in the late thirteenth century.

[16] Techniques of reiteration and of *enchaînement* to the theme established in the initial stanza.

The unexpected discovery of twenty two-to-four-line *cancioncillas*, written in Mozarabic language, lent support to Menendez Pidal's theory. The *cancioncillas*, or *jarchas*, dated around 1040, had a function similar to the villancico without glossing stanzas. They served as closing stanzas to the *muwassaha* or *moaxajas*, name given to certain Hebrew and Arabic poems. The most widely accepted theory at present, which has been endorsed mainly by S. M. Stern, Menendez Pidal, and Dámaso Alonso, is that the Spanish villancicos, the *cantigas de amigos* and the Mozarabic *jarchas* are all branches of the same traditional Iberian lyric.[17]

The discovery of the Mozarabic *jarchas* affected the theory proposed by the Arabic scholar Julián Ribera. Ribera hypothesized the existence of a primitive Spanish lyric which would have influenced Arabic poetry and helped to create the *muwassaha* and the *zejel*. In Ribera's view, the *zejel*, which appears toward the end of the ninth century, had become the metrical source of the *cantigas* and villancicos.[18] Since no examples of *zejel* music are known, attempts to determine a musical influence on the structure of *cantigas* and villancicos have been viewed with reservation.[19] Without diminishing the importance of the *zejel* and its possible influence on the development of European and particularly Provençal poetry, philologists and literary historians have shifted their interest to the *jarcha* as a more plausible source of influence on the development of the Iberian poetic lyric.

The rise of the *cancioncillas* into the mainstream of Spanish poetry and music was the result of the interest in popular forms of expression manifested by poets and musicians. This interest probably began at the Neapolitan court of Alfonso V of Aragon, where Carvajales was the court poet and Suero de Ribera had previously served. From the Neapolitan court, interest most likely extended to the Castilian and Navarran courts. The impact of these *cancioncillas* in the learned milieu can be measured by the large number of erudite writers and major composers who imitated their popular style.[20] Although a few glossed villancicos of the popular tradition have been preserved,[21] most of the existing compositions found in the Renaissance sources consist of the initial villancico followed by stanzas in the learned lyric style of the time. It can be conjectured, therefore, that poets and musicians used, as a point of departure for their own compositions, unappended villancicos, or villancicos separated from their glossing stanzas.

---

[17] Sanchez Romeralo, *Villancico*, pp. 343-52.

[18] Julián Ribera, *Music in Ancient Arabia and Spain*, trans. and abridged by Eleanor Hague and Marion Seffingwell (California: Stanford University Press, 1929), p. 159.

[19] Isabel Pope, "Musical and Metrical Form of the Villancico," *Annales Musicologiques* 2 (1954): pp. 212-14.

[20] Sanchez Romeralo, *Villancico*, pp. 50-51.

[21] Margit Frenk Alatorre, "Glosas de tipo popular en la antigua lírica," *Nueva Revista de Filología Hispánica* 12 (1958): 301-34. For the study of the textual relation between the villancico and its glosses, 164 examples were used.

Some of these *cancioncillas* became so popular that they were repeatedly collected in their original or varied forms. Sanchez Romeralo has traced the following villancico through various sources:[22]

> Enemiga le soy madre
> a aquel caballero yo
> Mal enemiga le soy.

> An enemy, mother
> of that gentleman am I
> His bad enemy am I.

This villancico appears in Luis Milan's *El Cortesano* (Valencia, 1561) as an anonymous and unattached composition. In the same format, it is ascribed to Juan del Encina[23] in a loose-leaf printed in Valladolid (1572). The same villancico with an added set of stanzas is presented in the *Cancionero Musical de Palacio* as an anonymous composition. In this new format and in the same *cancionero*, it has been compiled as Peñalosa's[24] *ensalada*, and ascribed to Juan de Espinosa.[25] The same initial *cancioncilla*, with stanzas similar to those in the above *cancionero*, has been included as an anonymous composition in Juan Linares' *Cancionero Flor de Enamorados* (Barcelona: 1562, 1608, 1645, 1547 and 1681). The villancico appears again with a set of stanzas different from those found in the *Cancionero Musical de Palacio*, as an anonymous composition in Juan Fernandez de Heredia's works (Valencia: 1562). Only in Lope de Sosa's *Villancicos de Navidad* (1603) is a different version of the initial stanza used to suit the occasion:

> Muy amiga le soy madre
> A aquel Jesús que nació
> más que a mí le quiero yo.[26]

> A good friend mother am I
> Of that Jesús who was born
> more than myself I love him.

---

22 Sanchez Romeralo, *Villancico*, pp. 19-21.

23 Juan del Encina (1468?-1529?), one of the most outstanding poets and musicians of his time, held the archdeaconship at the Malaga Cathedral from 2 April 1509 until 21 February 1519.

24 Francisco de Peñalosa (c. 1470-1528) was a protégé of Ferdinand V and Pope Leo X. Many of his Latin works have been preserved in various sources and eleven of his villancicos are compiled in the *Cancionero Musical de Palacio*.

25 There is not enough data indicating that Juan Espinosa, the composer of the villancicos numbers 4 and 202 in the *Cancionero Musical de Palacio*, is the same Juan Espinosa, writer of three theoretical treatises. From Robert Stevenson, *Spanish Music in the Age of Columbus* (The Hague: Martinus Nijhoff, 1960), p. 93.

26 Sanchez Romeralo, *Villancico*, p. 21.

Sanchez Romeralo's tracing of this particular villancico confirms the anonymity of the initial *cancioncilla*. It can be assumed that none of the authors mentioned above wrote the initial *cancioncilla*. Therefore, the authorship attributed to the villancico in various sources could correspond either to the composer of the music or to the writer of the stanzas attached to the initial *cancioncilla*. Asenjo Barbieri asserts that in the compositions of the *Cancionero Musical de Palacio*, the author's name normally refers to the composer rather than to the poet. However, he points out that the music and the text of some compositions could have been produced by the same person, because most of the musicians and poets of that time "were truly troubadours, who sang their lyric poetry accompanying themselves with the lute, *vihuela* or guitar."[27]

In the middle of the fifteenth century, then, the word villancico and similar terms began to be used in the Castilian court to designate songs of popular tradition which were sung and composed by the *villanos*. During the late fifteenth and sixteenth centuries, interest in the popular lyric on the part of literary men was manifested in three directions:

- Poets imitated closely the theme and language of traditional compositions.
- Poets used the traditional *cancioncilla* as a point of departure for their own glossing stanzas of courtly or popular character.
- Poets centered their attention on the brevity of the unattached *cancioncilla*, which was identified as the villancico, and especially on the irregularity of the number of syllables of its verses, one of them usually being a *pié quebrado*, or shorter verse (truncated verse). They retained the basic structure of the traditional *cancioncilla*, but by regularizing the length of its verses, they created a new poetic form—the *villancico cortés* or "courtly" villancico.

The most representative type of villancico of the late fifteenth and early sixteenth centuries consists of an initial stanza of three octosyllabic verses or two octosyllabic verses with a middle verse of *pié quebrado* (8/4/8). According to the practices of the literary lyric, this initial stanza, or *estribillo* (refrain), was followed by one or more glossing stanzas, or coplas.[28]

---

[27] *Cancionero musical de los siglos XV y XVI*, (Buenos Aires: Editorial Schapire, 1949), p. 9. Francisco Asenjo Barbieri was responsible for the first publication of the *Cancionero Musical de Palacio* and the first modern transcription of the music. The first edition was published in Madrid in 1890.

[28] A type of popular lyric composition which was also used by the learned poets. During the Middle Ages, Renaissance and even in later periods, the term *coplas* included a variety of strophic structures. Today, the term is almost exclusively restricted to the lyrics of popular songs.

The *coplas* consist of two sections: the first, generally a *cuarteta*[29] or *redondilla*,[30] rhymes differently from the *estribillo* and constitutes the *mudanza*, or change; the second section comprises the same number of verses as the *estribillo*. One or more of these verses serves as an *enlace*, or link with the *mudanza* and the others as a *vuelta*, or return to the rhyme of the *estribillo*.[31] Within the formal courtly lyric, the ABB and the AbB *pié quebrado* rhyme structure of the *estribillo* is a novelty, but the most outstanding characteristic is the relationship between the *coplas* and the initial *estribillo*.

		Rhyme	Rhyme
Estribillo		A	A
		B	B
		B	B
	Mudanza	C	C
		D	D
Copla		C	C
		D	C
	Enlace	D	C
	Vuelta	B	B
		B	B

In similar formats, the villancico maintained its supremacy as the national form of popular and learned expression until the end of the sixteenth century. During this century, however, the uninterrupted interaction between the popular and erudite poetry permitted two genres of the popular tradition, the *coplas*, and more powerfully, the new *seguidilla*,[32] to exert a great influence in the literary milieu. The practices of reiteration and glossing as techniques for strophic development began to lose ground. Toward the end of the sixteenth century, the *coplas* and the *seguidillas*, considered to be strophic variations of the villancico, emerged as forms of expression more suitable to the new literary taste and style.

Examples of villancicos with both poetry and music are first found in five Peninsular *cancioneros*. The compilation periods of the *cancioneros* correspond approximately to the reign of the Catholic kings:

1. *Cancionero de Sevilla* or *Cancionero Musical de la Biblioteca Columbina*, sign. 7-1-28. This manuscript, entitled

---

[29] A four-verse stanza with an ABAB rhyme.

[30] A stanza of four octosyllabic verses with ABBA rhyme.

[31] For a more extensive presentation of the development and formal structure of the fifteenth and sixteenth centuries' villancicos, see Sanchez Romeralo, *Villancico*, Chapter III.

[32] A seven verse stanza, of which the first four verses constitute the *copla* and the last three the refrain, or *estribillo*. Early examples of *seguidillas* can be found in the *Cancionero de Herberay des Essarts*.

Cantilenas vulgares puestas en música por varios españoles,[33] was copied at the end of the fifteenth century and probably contains the earliest examples of the traditional villancicos with music.

    2.   *Cancionero Musical de Segovia*, at the Biblioteca Capitular de Segovia, without signature. Also a manuscript from the fifteenth century, it has remained unpublished. Only folios 207-26 are available, and its contents and a concordance appear in Higinio Anglés' *La Música en la Corte de los Reyes Católicos.*[34]

    3.   *Cancionero Musical de Palacio* at the Biblioteca Nacional de Madrid, sign. 2-1-5. This manuscript, compiled in the last years of the fifteenth century and early years of the sixteenth century, was first edited by Francisco Asenjo Barbieri in 1892 under the title of *Cancionero Musical Español de los siglos XV y XVI*. It was re-edited in 1947-1951 by Higinio Anglés under the title of *La Música en la Corte de los Reyes Católicos* II and III.

    4.   *Cancionero Musical de Barcelona*, at the Biblioteca Central of Barcelona, M.S. 454. Only folios 120, 143v-144, 15v., 1-1v-1 6, and 1 9v-180 are available. This manuscript, compiled in the late fifteenth and early sixteenth centuries, is still unpublished. Its content and concordance appear in Higinio Anglés' *La Música en la Corte de los Reyes Católicos.*[35] A discussion of its contents and the transcription of a few pieces can be found in Felipe Pedrell's *Catálech de la Bibliotecca Musical de la Diputació de Barcelona.*[36]

    5.   *Cancionero Musical de Elvas* or *Cancionero Musical e Poetico da Biblioteca Publia Hortensia*, Elvas, Portugal, sign. 119-3. The manuscript belongs to the early part of the sixteenth century. It has been edited by Manuel Joaquim.[37]

    Although secular and religious villancicos are found in the *cancioneros* of the late fifteenth and early sixteenth centuries,[38] the secular ones were more predominant. However, the religious villancicos, particularly those related to Christmas subjects, began to be

---

[33] An early study of this manuscript was presented in Higinio Anglés, "Die Spanische Liedkunst im 15. und em anfang des 16. Jahrhunderts," *the Theodor Kroyer Festschrift*. (Regensburg: 1933). The index of its contents appears in Higinio Anglés' *La Música en la Corte de los Reyes Católicos*, *Monumentos de la Musica Española*, 1, (Madrid: Consejo Superior de Investigaciones Científicas, 1941), pp. 103-6. An important study of its content has been made by Robert Stevenson in *Spanish Music in the Age of Columbus*, pp. 206-64. A recent edition of this *cancionero* has been prepared by Miguel Querol Gavaldá under the title of *El Cancionero Musical de la Colombina*, (Barcelona: Consejo Superior de Investigaciones Científicas, 1971).

[34] *Monumentos de la Música Española*, 1. (Madrid: Consejo Superior de Investigaciones Científicas, 1947) pp. 106-12.

[35] *Ibid.*, pp. 112-15.

[36] Vol. 2 (Barcelona: 1908-1909), p. 155ff.

[37] (Coimbra: Tipografía de Atlántida, 1940).

[38] There are thirty religious villancicó included in the *Cancionero Musical de Palacio.*

performed in churches and monasteries during the singing of the Office Hours between the responsories of Matins.

The texts of the secular villancicos often expressed feelings of love, or dealt with events of daily life or special occasions. The subject of love was treated in a variety of ways. In the courtly villancicos it was usually expressed by praising the physical and spiritual qualities of the beloved woman *(elogio)*; by showing unbearable suffering and asking for the loved one's mercy *(recuesta)*; by complaining about love and lovers *(lamentación)*; and by vowing eternal fidelity.

The desire to escape the social and intellectual milieu was manifested in a search for pastoral innocence and a return to nature. Bucolic villancicos tell of love between young shepherds and shepherdesses, *zagal* and *zagala*; of courtly gentlemen disguised as peasants, who meet beautiful shepherdesses; or of a poet who listens to a shepherdess singing a villancico. Another pastoral love theme, which came from the Galician-Portuguese tradition, was that of a brave and strong *serranilla*, or mountain girl, who is met by a nobleman or hunter lost in the sierra. The women in these bucolic villancicos are often identified with fictional names such as Mengua, Pascuala, or Dominguilla.

The text of the early religious villancicos was particularly related to the Christmas season. During the sixteenth century, however, villancicos began to be written in praise of the Blessed Virgin Mary, the Saints, and in celebrations of other feasts of the Church.

The music of the secular and religious villancicos of the late fifteenth and early sixteenth centuries consists of two parts. The initial stanza, or *estribillo*, is sung to the first part of the music. The number of poetic lines of the *estribillo* (couplet, tercet, or quatrain) is matched by the number of melodic phrases. The *mudanza* of the *copla* is sung to the second part of the music. This part is made up of one or two melodic phrases, which are repeated to accommodate the two or four verses of the *mudanza*. The *enlace* and the *vuelta*, the latter rhyming with or repeating the last verse or verses of the *estribillo*, are sung to the music of the *estribillo*. Thus, the return of the first part of the music does not coincide with the return to the rhyme of the *estribillo*. Isabel Pope pointed out that the asymmetry produced between the repetition of the musical material and the delayed repetition of the poetic rhyme gives unity to the form by avoiding a sharp division of the material sections.[39]

---

[39] "Musical and Metrical Form of the Villancico," *Annales Musicologiques* 2 (1954): 202. Her scholarly article is one of the most important studies of early villancicos, especially of those contained in the *Cancionero Musical de Palacio*.

		Rhyme	Music	
Estribillo		a	a	A
		b	b	
		b	c	
	Mudanza	c	d	B
		d	e	
Copla		c	d	B
		d	e	
	Enlace	d	a	A
	Vuelta	b	b	
		b	c	

The villancico of the fifteenth and sixteenth centuries was a composition scored for voice or voices with or without instrumental accompaniment. The villancicos included in the earlier sources are usually three-to-four part settings. Some were probably performed by soloists with instrumental accompaniment.[40] The vocal parts move stepwise and are maintained within the octave range. Most villancicos give a chordal feeling although some imitation is found, especially in the opening measures. They are generally written in duple meter with occasional changes to triple meter. The text setting is predominantly syllabic, and the rhythmic patterns tend to enhance the accents of the words.[41]

The *Cancionero de Upsala*, which presents the musical trends from the years 1520 to 1540, reveals a new style in the development of the villancico. Under Netherlandish influence, the composers of villancicos often used text repetition for contrapuntal elaboration and expansion of the musical material.[42]

According to Miguel Querol Gavaldá, the development of the fifteenth and sixteenth century villancicos concludes around 1570. He states that the majority of the compositions included in the *Cancionero Musical de Medinaceli* are madrigals.[43] The influence of the madrigal style had been manifested a decade earlier in Juan Vásquez' *Recopilación de Sonetos y Villlancicos a quatro y a cinco*.[44]

During the sixteenth century, many villancicos were composed for soloists accompanied by lute or by the fashionable *vihuela de mano*.[45]

---

[40] Isabel Pope, "Villancico," *Die Musik in Geschichte und Gegenwart* 13 (Kassel: Bárenreiter-Verlag, 1966).

[41] Sister Teresita Espinosa, "Selected Unpublished Villancicos of Padre Antonio Soler..." 2 vols. (Ph.D. dissertation, University of Southern California, 1969) 1: 131-32.

[42] Isabel Pope, "Villancico," pp. 1629-30.

[43] *Cancionero Musical de la Casa de Medinacelli II, Monumentos de la Musica Española*, v. 9. (Barcelona: Consejo Superior de Investigaciones Científicas, 1950), p. 9.

[44] Higinio Anglés, ed., *Monumentos de la Música Española*, v. 4 (Barcelona: Consejo Superior de Investigaciones Científicas, 1946), p. 11.

[45] Sister Teresita Espinosa, "Villancicos of Padre Antonio Soler," p. 135.

Composers generally wrote several settings for the same villancico. The variety of settings was designed to provide opportunity for the vocalist and instrumentalist to demonstrate their taste and ability.[46] The popularity of the villancico also influenced the field of instrumental music. Composers borrowed villancico melodies and wrote instrumental variations and keyboard compositions in imitative counterpoint.[47]

The most renowned Spanish composers wrote secular and religious villancicos. A chronological list based on the appearance of their compositions in *cancioneros* and music collections of the late fifteenth and sixteenth centuries, includes:

> Pedro Escobar
> Juan del Encina
> Juan Ponce
> Jacobus Milarte
> Francisco Millan
> Badajoz
> Juan Ponce
> Juan Vásquez
> Mateo Flecha
> Pedro de Pastrana
> Diego Garcon
> Juan Navarro
> Ginés de Morata
> Antonio Cebrián
> Luis de Narvaez
> Enrique de Valderrábano
> Diego Pisador
> Miguel de Fuenllana
> Esteban Daza
> Alonso Mudarra

The subject matter of the villancico changed over time. What began in the secular realm gradually became a vital part of the religious life of the people. Toward the end of the sixteenth century and in succeeding centuries, the religious villancico began to be widely cultivated and eventually prevailed over the secular form.

During the seventeenth and eighteenth centuries, secular villancicos with subject matter similar to that of earlier secular villancicos continued to be performed. Although the author of the text was frequently kept anonymous, many were leading Spanish poets such as Lope de Vega (1562-1635) and Francisco Quevedo (1580-1645).

The text of the religious villancicos covered a wide range of subject matters. The Christmas villancicos, which became the predominant type during the seventeenth and eighteenth centuries,

---

[46] Emilio Pujol, ed., Luys de Narvaez' *Los seys libros del Delphin de Música, Monumentos de la Música Española*, v. 3. (Barcelona: Consejo Superior de Investigaciones Científicas, 1945), p. 48.

[47] Sister Teresita Espinosa, "Villancicos of Padre Antonio Soler," p. 138.

usually emphasized the divinity of the Child and the meaning of his Birth.[48] Villancicos with Marian texts containing praises, prayers and implorations were generally sung at the Feast of the Immaculate Conception. Religious villancicos were also written in celebration of Saint Days and of other major religious occasions, such as Easter and Corpus Christi. In some churches and monasteries, villancicos were performed at Mass replacing the gradual and offertory.

Some religious institutions employed poets to write villancicos for all the required occasions. Often the text of the villancico was published and distributed among the parishioners. Because the custom throughout Spain and its domain was to publish the text without the name of the author, most writers of religious villancico texts, like their secular counterparts, have remained largely unknown. In general, literary quality of the villancicos of these centuries is beneath their musical value. Because religious texts often became unrefined, satiric, and roguish, they had to be constantly reviewed by the chapelmaster responsible for setting them to music, or by the corresponding ecclesiastical authorities.

The texts of most secular and religious villancicos were written in the learned literary style of the seventeenth and eighteenth centuries. Others, however, with a broader public appeal, including some performed at church feasts, were written in plain language or dialects typical to some regions of the Iberian Peninsula, especially Galicia. A few were still written in Latin, Italian, and Portuguese, and others in the dialect of the Blacks of the Spanish colonies of the New World.

The incorporation of the villancico within the liturgical service was not without criticism. On 11 June 1596, Phillip II issued a royal decree prohibiting the singing of villancicos or any other composition in the vernacular in the Royal Chapel.[49] Although Pedro Ceron approved the singing of villancicos during the religious services, he pointed out in *El Melopeo y el Maestro* (1613), that their performance seemed to distract the congregation from the devotion of the service, especially when villancico texts were in another language. He asked if the House of God should become a recreation place and complained that people who never came to Mass were always there when villancicos were performed.[50]

The practice of singing villancicos was well established in most churches and monasteries by the early part of the seventeenth century. Vicente Ripollés reports that at the Valencia Cathedral, villancicos became an integral part of religious services during the second or third decade of the seventeenth century.[51] The Malaga Cathedral was perhaps one of the last churches to incorporate the singing of villancicos into the

---

[48] Sister Mary Paulina St. Amour, *A Study of the Villancico up to Lope de Vega* (Washington, D.C.: The Catholic University of America, 1940), p. 44.

[49] Jaime Moll, "Los Villancicos cantados en la Capilla Real a fines del siglo XVI y principios del siglo XVII," *Anuario Musical* 25 (1970): 81-96.

[50] *Ibid.*

[51] *El villancico i la cantata del segle XVIII a Valéncia.* (Barcelona: Institut de'Estudis Catalana—Biblioteca Catalunya, 1935), p. v.

service (c. 1648), but it was also one of the last to abandon this practice (1798).

Toward the end of the sixteenth century, the musical structure of the villancico began to undergo radical changes. In the seventeenth century it emerged as a composition with few links to its earlier counterpart. The villancicos of the seventeenth and eighteenth centuries present a variety of forms and styles, but they all had common features that distinguished them from the earlier types. The new villancico consisted of two or more independent and contrasting structural parts. Under the influence of the vocal and instrumental baroque style, and the fashionable music of the Spanish theater, the traditional *estribillo-coplas* format is expanded and transformed. The vocal texture of this villancico includes one or more soloists and frequently a four-to-twelve-voice chorus. The instrumental accompaniment includes: continuo, continuo with strings, and continuo with strings and winds.

Of the many facets of this new villancico, there is one in particular that presents the most challenging departure from the villancico of the fifteenth and sixteenth centuries. It became known in the latter part of the seventeenth and into the eighteenth century as *cantata* or *cantada*. This is the type which is generally associated with the villancico form of this period. This extended multi-sectional work, written in a more learned style, usually includes one aria and two recitatives. Further details of this type of villancico are contained in Chapter VI.

The study of the villancico is far from being completed. Before the development of this form can be clearly understood, it will be necessary to gain more information from the abundant Spanish musical sources, particularly of the seventeenth and eighteenth centuries. Our lack of knowledge about this important Spanish form of literary and musical expression is probably due to the scarcity of music publications in Spain in past centuries. In regard to this situation, Dr. Robert Stevenson says:

> ...their [Spanish composers] failure to circulate, and their failure to publish and propagandize their works abroad may account for the obscurity that prevents even their names from entering standard histories and encyclopedias.[52]

---

[52] *Renaissance and Baroque Music in the Americas*, p. 39.

CHAPTER VI

THE VILLANCICOS OF JUAN FRANCÉS DE IRIBARREN

The religious villancico was at the peak of its popularity when Juan Francés de Iribarren was actively composing at Malaga. Constant demands on chapelmasters to compose new villancicos for performance at the various liturgical feasts may account for Iribarren's tremendous output in this musical form. A tally of his compositions taken from the *Inventario Musical de 1770* disclosed about 550 villancicos. Of these works, 505 have been preserved in manuscript form in the Malaga Cathedral's archives. For this study of Iribarren's villancicos, forty-seven compositions have been selected from those available at the Cathedral. This selection, representative of Iribarren's production in this media, was based on dates of compositions, occasions of performance, number of structural parts, vocal scoring, instrumentation, text, and style.

The dates of the selected villancicos extend from 1733 to 1760; that is, from the year that Iribarren assumed his position at Malaga until the year that his villancicos were last recorded in the 1770 musical inventory. Three of these compositions were written for performance on Immaculate Conception Day; seven for the feast of the Blessed Sacrament; and thirty-seven at Christmas. The greater availability of Christmas villancicos can be attributed to the fact that sets of eight or nine villancicos were sung at that particular celebration; sets of only four seemed to have been performed at the Immaculate Conception Day; and a varying number of villancicos during the Blessed Sacrament festivity.

The villancico sung in Spanish churches and monasteries during the seventeenth and eighteenth centuries differs noticeably from the villancicos cultivated during the late fifteenth and sixteenth centuries. Unlike the earlier form, which was primarily a single movement vocal composition with or without instrumental accompaniment, the later villancico appears as a composite form with continuo and instrumental accompaniment.

Iribarren's villancicos are written for one to eight voices with continuo and instrumental accompaniment. An examination of the forty-seven selected villancicos revealed the following vocal scoring:

1	solo
3	solo and chorus
6	duets
3	duets and chorus
1	trio
11	trio and chorus
8	quartet
2	quintet
12	two choruses

The compositions for soloist are one villancico for soprano and three for alto. The vocal combinations for duets are first and second soprano, soprano and alto, soprano and tenor, and alto and tenor. Trios are scored for soprano, alto, and tenor. Quartets consists of first and second soprano, alto and tenor. One of the quintets is written for first, second, and third soprano, alto and tenor; the other, for first and second soprano, alto, and first and second tenor. In the villancicos for two choruses, the first chorus keeps the quartet setting while the second chorus is always scored for soprano, alto, tenor, and bass. In the setting for soloist or soloists and chorus, the solo parts are always designated as belonging to the first chorus.

Of the forty-seven villancicos available, only one is scored for voices and continuo without instrumental accompaniment. The remaining forty-six are all scored for other instruments in addition to the continuo, for which sometimes the organ, or the harp or a stringed instrument is indicated. For the orchestration of his villancicos, Iribarren used *flauta traversa* (transverse flute), *flauta dulce* (recorder), *flautino* (small recorder or piccolo), clarinet, oboe, *chirimía* (oboe family), *bajón* (bassoon family), *bajoncillo* (small bajón), *trompa* (French horn or trumpet),[1] *clarín* (high pitched trompa), and violin.

An examination of the available villancicos revealed, in addition to the continuo part, the following instrumental scoring:[2]

3	for *bajoncillos*
15	for violins
1	for *bajoncillo* and recorder
1	for violin and piccolo
1	for violin and recorder
3	for violins and flute
2	for violins and oboe
1	for violins and *clarines*
9	for violins and *trompas*
1	for violins, flute and *trompas*
1	for violins, oboe and piccolo
1	for violins, oboe and *chirimías*
1	for violins, oboe and *clarines*
1	for violins, *clarines* and *trompas*
1	for violins, flute, *bajón* and *bajoncillo*
1	for violins, oboe, *trompa* and recorder
1	for violins, oboe, *trompas* and *clarines*

Chirimías, bajónes and bajoncillos used to be standard instruments in the Spanish church orchestras of the previous centuries. The chirimía is described in the *Enciclopedia Universal Ilustrada* as a woodwind instrument of different lengths, similar to the clarinet and perhaps of Arabic origin. In its early stage of development, the *chirimía* had nine holes bored in its side wall; of the nine holes, only six were closed by

---

[1] The range of the trompas used by Iribarren is discussed in the following chapter.

[2] See Appendix F.

the fingers.[3] Felipe Pedrell agrees with this structural description of the instrument, but he places it within the oboe family.[4] In support of Pedrell's classification is Pablo Nasarre's description of the *chirimía* as a double reed instrument.[5] In Iribarren's villancicos, the *chirimía* and the oboe are scored in the same range.

The *bajón* is usually identified with the bassoon and the bajoncillo with a higher-pitched bassoon. Santiago Katsner points out, however, that in a list of instrumentalists performing at the Badajoz Cathedral in 1700, both a *bajón* and a bassoon player are included. Therefore, he suggests that the two terms refer to two different instruments.[6]

Sources do not agree in their definition of the *trompa*. Some of them describe it as an instrument similar to the horn; others, as an instrument akin to the modern trumpet. Pedrell presents it as similar to the horn, but indicates that the term has created a great deal of confusion. It is applied not only to the horn and trumpet, but also to other instruments very different from those two.[7] The word *trompa* was probably used in the eighteenth century for various brass instruments.

Iribarren favored the violin above all other instruments for his villancicos, particularly those written before 1740. The use of the violin, although amply accepted in the performance of eighteenth-century sacred music, still raised controversy among theorists and critics of music. One critic who presented a rather conservative attitude for his time was Benito Feijoo (1676-1764), a Benedictine monk and contemporary of Iribarren. He criticized large instrumentation for the music of the church, being particularly antagonistic to the use of the violin during liturgical services. He also condemned the abuse of altered and fast notes in the writing for this instrument and complained about its sound saying that

> ...sus [violin] chillidos, aunque armoniosos son chillidos y excitan una viveza como pueril en nuestros espiritus...especialmente en este tiempo, que los que componen para violines ponen estudios en hacer las composiciones tan subidas que el ejecutor vaya a dar al puente con los dedos.[8]

> ...its [violin] squeaks, although harmonious, are only squeaks, and they raise a puerile excitement in our spirits...particularly because those who compose for violin at this time put such an emphasis on high pitched compositions that the performer cannot avoid hitting the bridge with his fingers.

---

[3] *Enciclopedia Universal Ilustrada*, 1958 ed., s.v. "Chirimía."

[4] *Diccionario técnico de la música*, 1894 ed., s.v. "Chirimía."

[5] *Escuela música según la práctica moderna*, (Saragoza: Talleres de Diego Larrumbe y Manuel Román, 1724 and 1723), 2 vols.

[6] "La música en la Catedral de Badajoz (años 1654-1764)." *Anuario Musical*, 18 (1963): 234.

[7] *Diccionario técnico de la música*, s.v. "Trompa."

[8] Cited by Tello, *Teoría Española de la música*, pp. 164-65.

In response to Feijoo's position, Estaquio Cerbellon de la Vera argued that chromaticism and fast passages used in moderation and taste enhance the harmony of religious compositions and are conducive to pious meditation and divine contemplation.[9]

Another opponent of Feijoo's writing was Juan Francisco Corona, concertmaster at Salamanca University. He stated that if Feijoo accepted the use of high-pitched instruments such as *chirimías, cornets* and oboes in the church, he would not condemn the playing of violins.[10] The transformation of the villancico from a single movement to a composite form coincided with the baroque trend toward structural expansion affecting most of the musical forms of that period. The *estribillo*, which in the traditional *estribillo-copla* scheme consisted of a two-to-four-line refrain, was increased in length by the addition of one or more stanzas to the refrain. The expansion of the *estribillo* brought as a consequence the independence of this element from the *coplas* and the transformation of the villancico from a short sectional composition into a larger two movement form. The independence of the *estribillo* from the *coplas* permitted combinations of these two movements with vocal and instrumental baroque forms, and with compositions unique to the Spanish musical idiom.

The inclusion of arias, recitatives, allegros, *tonadillas, seguidillas*, and other forms used either as additional or substitutive movements for the *estribillo* and the *coplas* was a matter of lasting controversy. One spokesman on this issue was Francisco de Sayas. He criticized the incorporation of fashionable secular and theatrical compositions into the religious compositions as flattering to the ear, but devoid of proper spiritual feeling.[11] Another spokesman, the Catalunian composer Francisco Valls (1665-1747), asserted that admitting forms of secular origin into the liturgy should not mean that the character of these compositions should be assimilated to the religious music.[12] In spite of continuous controversy among musicians and critics of music, religious

---

[9] Cited by Tello, *Teoría Española de la música*, p. 165.

[10] Cited in *Ibid.*, p. 184. Corona's *Aposenta anticrítico desde donde se ve representar la gran comedia, que en su Theatro crítico regalóp al pueblo el R.R. P.M. Feijoo, contra la música moderna y uso de los violines en los templos.* (Salamanca: Imprenta de la Santa Cruz, 1726). The publication was dedicated to Diego Fernando de Contreras, archdeacon of the Salamanca Cathedral, at the time that Iribarren was working in that city.

[11] *Música canónica*, cited by Tello, *Teoría Española de la Música*, p. 239.

[12] Tello, *Teoría Española de la Música*, pp. 550-79. Valls served as chapelmaster at the Gerona Cathedral, Mataró Parroquial Church, Santa María del Mar in Barcelona and Barcelona Cathedral. His unpublished book, "Mapa armónico-práctico, breve resumen de las principales reglas de música..." was finished about 1747.

villancicos were cultivated during the seventeenth and eighteenth centuries in a variety of structures and styles.

A general survey of Iribarren's villancicos available at the Malaga Cathedral reveals that his villancicos range from two to five movements. His two-movement compositions are by far the most numerous, although those in three, four, and five movements are well represented. Among the villancicos selected for this study, thirty-one are structured in two movements, seven in three, two in four, and seven in five movements.

Iribarren's villancicos in two movements have standard overall form. The first movement, which is designated as the *estribillo* until 1752, and after that date as *entrada*, allegro, or introduction, is always based on a poetic form with a refrain or *estribillo*. The second movement, called *coplas*, is usually set to a text consisting of three or more stanzas. Of all the villancicos examined, the refrain of the first movement is repeated after each one of the stanzas of the *coplas* movement. The unification of the two movements through the repetition of the refrain suggests that this type of villancico, to a certain extent, preserved a structure akin to the *estribillo-copla* scheme of the late fifteenth- and sixteenth-century villancico.

An examination of Iribarren's thirty-one villancicos in two movements shows the following formal structures.

Estribillo	Entrada
Coplas	Coplas
1749 A Belén pastorcillas*	1758 Abandonados cautivos
1749 Así, al chocorrotiya	1754 Batillo con su mujer
1736 Ay que alegre festivo	1755 Bato y Pascuala contentos
1742 Cantando y bailando	1752 Ea, ea, Anfiso alegre
1750 Digo que noche de cantarla	1759 Esta noche es nochebuena
1743 Helmana Flancisca	1752 Las tiernas pastorcillas
1738 Montados en sus esdrújulos	1755 Los plateros de Belén
1745 Oiga Señor mío	1754 Un siciliano festivo
1749 Seguidillas muchachos	
1736 Vamos corriendo a buscar	
1740 Vamos culendita	

Allegro
Coplas
1760 Un pastor muy jacarero
1759 Vaya, vaya jacarilla
1757 Ya que el Niño hermoso

---

* Villancico transcribed in this book.

53

Entrada-Allegro	Introducción-Allegro
Coplas	Coplas
1755 Los gallegos enfadados	1760 Cerrando la mogiganga
1759 Un gallardo portugués	1760 Porque en la entrada festiva

Introducción-Estribillo
Coplas
1736 El herrador de Belén
1749 Hacer quiere una comedia Gil
1752 Las zagalas de Belén*
1750 Para divertir al Niño

The overall structure of Iribarren's villancicos in three movements consists of a variable first movement always followed by a recitative and an aria. The presence of recitatives and arias within the structure of the villancicos in three or more movements has brought about the comparison of this form with the church cantata and the English anthem. In Iribarren's three-movement villancicos, the *coplas* movement is generally omitted and the *estribillo* or *estribillo*-like movement is substituted by an *entrada*. Unlike those included in the two-movement villancicos, this *entrada* often lacks textual and musical refrains.

Of the seven following examples of Iribarren's villancicos in three movements, six open with an *entrada* and only one preserves the *coplas* as first movement.

Entrada	Coplas
Recitative	Recitative
Aria	Aria
1754 Alados celestiales*	1754 Un danzante mi Niño
1740 Cuando vayando vuelven	
1756 Las aves acordes*	
1754 Las hojas se mueven	
1758 Oh! que halagueña canción	
1753 Zagales corred	

The two four-movement villancicos selected for this study consist of *estribillo*, recitative, aria and finale. However, the sequence of movements of these two compositions may not necessarily represent the formal structure of all the Iribarren's villancicos in four movements, although recitative and aria seem to be nuclear movements.

---

* Villancicos transcribed in this book.

The two examples available have the following structure:

Estribillo
Recitative
Aria
Final
1740   Corriendo zagales
1733   Pues eterno el día

Iribarren's five-movement villancicos consist of a variable opening movement followed by three fixed movements in the order of recitative, aria, recitative, and a variable closing movement. In some of the compositions, the first and fifth movement correspond respectively to the structure of the *estribillo* and *coplas* movements found in his two-movement villancicos. If both movements are present in the villancico, they are bound together textually in spite of their outmost position.

The seven selected compositions show the following arrangement of movements:

Estribillo	Introducción-Estribillo
Recitative	Recitative
Aria	Aria
Recitative	Recitative
Allegro	Gigue
1736 Prisioneros alentad	1738 Triste lamenta Israel
1749 Reparad zagales	
Introducción	Introducción
Recitative	Recitative
Aria	Aria
Recitative	Recitative
Pastorela	Final Airoso
1736 A Belén caminad pastorcillos*	1738 Recoged las velas
Entrada	Entrada
Recitative	Recitative
Aria	Aria
Recitative	Recitative
Final Allegro	Canción
1740 Delicioso clavel	1740 Huyendo la ruina

Iribarren's villancicos, for the most part, are written in major keys. Prevalence is given to the sharp keys with up to three accidentals in the key signature. Conversely, the keys of a, d, and g are used for villancicos in minor tonalities.

Only the two-movement villancico, as a rule, has both movements in the same key. The repetition of the refrain of the first movement after each of the *coplas* movement, may account largely for the use of a common key for both movements. Of the thirty-one compositions of this type which were examined, twenty-nine had both movements in the same key. In the two remaining examples, the movements are written in related keys. This coincides with the fact that the first movement of these villancicos does not have a refrain to be repeated in the *coplas*.

The movements of villancicos in three or more movements are usually written in different keys. Of the sixteen examples examined, only two of the villancicos in three movements have all movements written in the same key. The harmonic-modulating scheme of the movements usually involves the standard changes of key, but occasionally the modulatory scheme moves by a whole tone upward. Regardless of the number of movements of the villancico, the first and last movements are written in the same key if they are textually bound.

Villancicos combine a variety of pieces of different character. To draw some conclusions about the type of compositions which Iribarren used as components for his villancicos and about his structural techniques, each of the movements constituting the forty-seven villancicos has been examined. A survey of the texts of these compositions was not intended, but it is difficult to overlook the interaction between words and musical settings. Therefore, comments on the texts complement the musical discussion whenever the texts show influence on the formal structure, rhythm, melody, harmony, tempo, or any other aspect of the compositions.

Estribillo:

Until 1752, the term *estribillo* appears in all of the opening movements of Iribarren's villancicos. With only two exceptions, all of the *estribillos* examined up to that date are based on poetic forms with refrains. After 1752, the use of the Spanish term for this form disappears and the opening movements are identified as introduction, *entrada*, or allegro. A closer examination of these movements reveals, however, that although the term *estribillo* was not retained in the later manuscripts, many of the movements labeled as introduction, *entrada*, or allegro present textual and musical characteristics analogous to those of the *estribillo* movements. Hence, to simplify matters, all opening movements presenting *estribillo*-like characteristics have been included under the general discussion of *estribillos*.

Iribarren's *estribillos* vary greatly in length. Those examined range from 40 to 150 measures. Usually the most extensive compositions belong to villancicos *de Calenda,* which are the most important villancicos sung at any occasion. Most *estribillos* are written in ternary meter. Binary or compound time signatures are indicated for only a few. No particular rhythmic patterns can be pointed out as pertinent to these movements, yet hemiola passages are often found at cadential points. Tempo mark specifications, ordered by the number of *estribillos* to which they apply, are allegro, airoso and vivo.

The number of vocal and instrumental parts used in the *estribillo* vary according to the type of villancico. But unlike other movements, the *estribillo* fully uses all of the vocal combinations as well as combinations of vocal and instrumental parts. *Estribillos*, for the most part, are written in major keys. Nevertheless, many retain modal characteristics whether the key signatures imply major or minor tonalities. Within the *estribillo* movements, modulations usually progress from the tonic key to the dominant and from a major key to its relative minor or vice versa. Harmonic progressions, as a rule, show more complexities in *estribillos* which are followed by recitative or aria movements.

Almost every *estribillo* examined is based either on a poetic form with an opening and closing refrain or a poetic form with the opening refrain repeated after each of the stanzas. However, in setting these two textual schemes to music, Iribarren skillfully avoided the restrictions of these two textual frames. Instead of producing standardized types of compositions, he used each type of poetic structure as a springboard for a variety of compositional procedures which resulted in a diversified and flexible musical treatment of the *estribillo* texts.

As the poetic form determines to a great extent the organization of the musical material, the *estribillo* movements have been classified below according to both textual and musical structure.

Type I. The text of these *estribillos* consists of an opening refrain followed by one or more stanzas. The refrain, regardless of the number of stanzas, is repeated only after the last stanza. All stanzas are sung to the same melody, which is different from the melody of the refrain.

	Text	Music
A	refrain	a
B	stanza(s)	b
A	refrain	a

Type II. The poetic form corresponds to that of Type I. As above, all stanzas are sung to the same melody, but the refrain and its repetition are sung to two different melodies.

	Text	Music
A	refrain	a
B	stanza(s)	b
A	refrain	c

Type III. The text structure of these *estribillos* also corresponds to Type I. The musical setting is strophic. However, while the refrain is always sung to the same melody, the stanzas are sung to variations of the refrain's music.

	Text	Music			Text	Music
A	refrain	a		A	refrain	a
B	stanza	a'	—or—	B	stanza	a'
A	refrain	a		C	stanza	a"
				D	stanza	a'''
				A	refrain	a

Type IV. In this two-stanza poetic form, the opening refrain is repeated after each of the stanzas. The first recurrence of the refrain is

57

set to a variation of the original music, the second to a different melody. Each stanza has its own musical setting. The music of the stanzas is different from that of the refrains.

	Text	Music
A	refrain	a
B	stanza	b
A	refrain	a'
C	stanza	c
A	refrain	d

Type V. The text of the two *estribillos* grouped under this heading belongs either to strophic forms without refrain, or to forms in which the repetition of the refrain has been omitted from the musical setting. Both compositions are through composed, that is, each stanza is set to different music.

	Text	Music
A	stanza	a
B	stanza	b
C	stanza, etc.	c, etc.

An interesting development of the estribillo, possibly related to the trend of structural expansion, is the insertion or addition of other musical forms. In the villancico "Hacer quiere una comedia Gil," a recitative is inserted between the refrain and the first stanza. In "El herrador de Belén," one recitative is inserted between the refrain and the first stanza, and the other after the first stanza and before the repetition of the refrain.

Another structural expansion observed in a large number of Iribarren's *estribillo* movements is the addition of one or sometimes two quatrains of a narrative character anticipating the subject matter or presenting the personages involved in the villancico text. These stanzas, indicated in the manuscripts as introduction, or *entradas*, are found either separated from the *estribillo* by a double bar line or incorporated into the movement.

In the analysis of the texts of the *estribillo* movements just presented, the introductory stanzas were considered simply as an introduction to the first movement, therefore they were not included in the structure of the main body of the *estribillo*. However, if these introductory stanzas are included as part of the text of the *estribillo* movement, the villancico could be considered as based on a *romance* text and not on a villancico text.

Since the late fifteenth century, both the villancico and the *romance*, another genuine poetic expression of the Spanish tradition, had been favored by poets and musicians. The *romance* of the fifteenth century consisted of four verses with assonant rhyme in the even-numbered verses. Each verse was set to a musical phrase, and each phrase was separated by a pause. In the sixteenth century, the *romance* was set to the same music. But the most important difference between the *romance* of the sixteenth century and the one of the previous century is that the last line of the strophe is repeated for conclusive effect.

The *romance*, as well as the villancico of the seventeenth century, was influenced by baroque trends of expansion. The length of the *romance* of this period is increased by adding a refrain different in meter and rhyme from that of the *romance*, to which *coplas* were often appended. It can be said, to a certain extent, that the *romance* was expanded by the addition of a villancico-type composition. From the earliest appearance of the villancico and the *romance*, these two musical-poetic forms have often been incorrectly designated.

The expanded form of the *romance* is found in many of Iribarren's *estribillo* movements. In setting these *romances* to music under the generic name of villancico, Iribarren often emphasized the introduction of the refrain and appended *coplas* by changing the meter and occasionally the tonality of the music as well. Thus, the *estribillo* became a two-section movement.

The textual and musical scheme for this *estribillo*-like movement is as follows:

	Text		Music
A	stanza(s)	romance	a
B	refrain	added material	b
C	stanza(s)		c
B	refrain		b

The above mentioned additional material generally consisted of *seguidillas, tonadillas, pastorales,* and *jácaras.* These were musical-poetic forms which reflected the nationalistic trends of the composers and were quite fashionable in the Spanish theater of the eighteenth century.

Seguidilla:

The *seguidilla* is one of the genuine manifestations of popular Spanish lyric poetry. It is the only form which contains generalized use of heptasyllabic verses. The *seguidilla* consists of a four-line copla and a three-line refrain. Lines one and three of the *copla* are heptasyllabic; lines two and four are pentasyllabic. In the refrain, which sometimes is deleted, lines one and three are pentasyllabic and line two is heptasyllabic.

The subject matter is always light, gay, or satiric, and occasionally includes some use of dialogue. *Seguidillas* found in Iribarren's villancicos are usually written in 6/8 time, in tempo allegro. A rhythmic pattern commonly used is:

Tonadilla:

The word *tonadilla* derives from *tono* and *tonada*, terms which designate a song. The term was first applied to melodies of prevailing lyrical character, which were sung at any place and for any occasion. The use of the term broadened in the seventeenth and eighteenth centuries to include all types of songs from the very popular to the most sophisticated aria. Narrowing the meaning of the term, *tonadilla* was singled out as a short song, usually with a refrain. These types of *tonadilas* are found in the *estribillo* movement of the villancicos of the eighteenth century.

Tonadillas began to be performed in the eighteenth century as theatrical *intermezzi*, accompanied by guitar, cello, or bass. These performances gave origin to the *tonadilla escénica*, which was generally based on events of Spanish life, and often satiric in its approach. The *tonadilla escénica* was staged for one or more characters and consisted of an introduction, in which the subject matter was usually presented by a female singer; *coplas*, which varied in the number of stanzas; and a *finale*, in which the commentaries on the plot were generally in *coplas* of *seguidillas*.[13]

The *tonadillas escénicas* were not only performed in public theaters, but also in the royal theater and in the homes of the Spanish aristocracy. The success of the *tonadilla escénica* is attested by the innumerable compositions available in archives and private libraries.

Iribarren's *tonadillas* are songs with a refrain. As such, they are incorporated into the *estribillo* movement of the villancico. *Tonadillas* present two possible textual and musical schemes. In the first, the text is repeated twice. One or two soloists sing the text for the first time and the same melody is harmonized by all vocal parts for the repetition.

Text	*Music*
A	a
A	a'

The second scheme includes two different strophes, each set to different music. They are separated, however, by the repetition of the same textual and musical refrain.

Text	*Music*
A	a
B	b
C	c
B	b

The *tonadilla* is usually set to different music than that of the *estribillo*, thus creating a two-section *estribillo* movement. In only one

---

[13] José Subirá, *Historia de la Música Teatral in España*, (Barcelona: Editorial Labor, 1945), pp. 144-51.

instance of the examples presented is the *tonadilla* incorporated into the *coplas* movement and it is placed between the *coplas* and the *respuestas*. The *tonadilla* is textually a narrative song, using various poetic forms, particularly *coplas* of *seguidillas*. Characters such as shepherds and shepherdesses, lads and lasses, are commonly introduced in this component of the villancico, identified by traditional ficticious names such as Bato and Pasquala. Influenced perhaps by the *tonadilla escénica*, the text is sometimes set in dialogue form. The popular character of these texts lends itself to the use of regional Peninsular dialects.

Tonadillas are written in ternary and compound meters with some characteristic rhythmic patterns such as:

It uses simple I-IV-V-I progressions. Modulations are usually restricted to the related keys, and augmented sixth chords are often employed in the modulatory passages. *Tonadillas* combine sounds imitative of animals, objects or instruments such as the bagpipe, with the more sophisticated vocalizations common to Italian operatic arias. This creates a blend of the traditional with learned or compositional devices of the period. *Tonadillas* are also composed upon a ground bass.

Jácaras:

The popularity of the *jácara* began with the writings of Juan del Encina (1468?-1529?). During the sixteenth and seventeenth centuries, the most common subjects of the *jácara* were love, happiness, and courtly matters. By the eighteenth century, *jácaras*, as well as other traditional Spanish musical-poetic forms, were performed as theatrical interludes, and were included as part of the *tonadilla escénica*.
Jácaras began to be used as religious compositions in the seventeenth century. Jerónimo de Cáncer y Velasco (159–?-1655)[14] wrote devout *jácaras* in dialogue form. In the available Iribarren examples, *jácaras* are included only in the two movement villancicos. If the *jácara* is used in the opening movement, part of the same *jácara* text is used in the *respuestas* of the *coplas* movement. Sometimes *jácaras* are used only for the *coplas* section of the *coplas* movement. *Jácaras* are written in 6/8 or 3/4 time signatures, in both major and minor keys. Tempo is generally marked allegro. A characteristic of these compositions is the use of phrases in the texts such as "vaya, vaya jacarilla," or "corra, corra, jacarilla." Another characteristic is the repetition of notes in the continuo line.

---

[14] See Emilio Cotarelo y Mori, *Colección de Entremeses, Loas, Bailes, Jácaras y Mojigangas desde fines del siglo XVI a mediados del XVIII*, (Madrid: Tipografía de la "Revista de archivos, bibliotecas y museos," (1911).

Pastorelas:

The *pastorela* has its origin in Provençal literature. The text usually consists of a dialogue between a shepherd and a shepherdess or between a gentleman and a shepherdess. The *pastorela* was a successful expression of Galician literature. It has been considered the precursor of the *serranilla*. In the eighteenth century, *pastorelas* were also included in the *tonadillas escénicas*.

Iribarren's *pastorelas* are lively compositions. With one exception, which is written in 3/4 time signature, the four remaining Iribarren *pastorelas* are written in 12/8 time. A common rhythmic pattern is:

Pastorelas are also used in the *coplas* section of the *coplas* movement. However, unlike the other Spanish musical poetic forms just examined, *pastorelas* are also used in aria movements.[15]

Entradas:

The terms *entrada*, introduction and allegro, as well as *estribillo*, are used to designate the first movement of Iribarren's villancicos. Some of the movements thus designated have the same structure as an *estribillo* movement, and have been discussed in the *estribillo* section. Therefore, only those movements which do not have *estribillo*-like characteristics shall be discussed here.

Of the nineteen *entrada* movements which appear in the forty-seven selected Iribarren villancicos, only seven were not *estribillo*-like, and one was a short introductory stanza to an allegro movement. The seven *entradas* which will be discussed here are based on poetic forms without refrain, and are included in the three-, four-, and five-movement villancicos.

Entradas are usually lengthy compositions. As in the opening movements of all the villancicos examined, *entradas* display all of the vocal and instrumental parts used in the score. The movement generally begins with a vocal and instrumental statement of the theme which will be used in the development of the movement. If this thematic material is presented only instrumentally, it is immediately restated by the vocal parts. In the more extended movements, soloistic and choral parts alternate with instrumental passages.

Tempo marks run the gamut from allegro to andante. In some of the movements there exists a change in tempo within the section. Time signatures indicate duple, ternary, and compound meters. No specific rhythmic pattern can be traced, although there seems to be a preference for dotted rhythms.

With one exception, all of the *entradas* examined are in major keys. The most common modulations are to dominant keys, with only a few to relative minor keys. Occasionally, passing chromatic

---

[15] See: Mía I. Gerhard, *La Pastorela*, (Assen, Holland: 1950).

modulations are introduced. The chord used most often for modulations is the diminished seventh. Vocalizations, word painting, and imitation are some of the compositional devices used in these movements. In general, the *entrada* makes use of more learned compositional procedures than those of the *estribillo*-like movements. They are consistent with the recitatives and arias included in the same villancico.

Allegro and Introduction:

The allegros found in the examined villancicos correspond to the *estribillo*-like movement. Some of the introduction movements are also *estribillo*-like; others are *entrada*-like. Therefore, these movements will not be discussed separately.

Although Iribarren uses a harmonic idiom in his opening movements, particularly in those of popular character, there is a constant resorting to contrapuntal techniques of imitation, and fragmentary alternation of notes or of passages. Iribarren also makes abundant use of word painting to convey subjective meanings of words and phrases, or to simulate natural sounds.

Coplas:

In keeping with the *estribillo-coplas* format of the traditional villancico, Iribarren used *coplas* as the closing movement for all his composition in two movements. *Coplas* movements seldom enter into the composition of villancicos in three movements. Only one of the compositions available in this type presents *coplas* as an opening movement. Movements specifically designated as *coplas* are not included in the four- and five-movement villancicos. However, some of the *pastorelas*, finales and allegros used as closing movements for these villancicos show the same formal structure of the *coplas* movements. Therefore, all movements which exhibit characteristics similar to those of the *coplas* movements, regardless of their designation, are included in the following discussion.

The texts of the *coplas* movements consist of several *coplas* or stanzas, and *respuestas* or answers, which are repeated after each *copla* and function as a refrain. The music of the *coplas* movements is composed of two parts, *coplas* are sung to the first part, and *respuestas* are sung to the second.

The word *coplas* was used as a generic term to describe stanzas representative of the Spanish lyric. *Coplas de arte mayor*, which refer to eight-line stanzas of twelve syllables each, were cultivated by learned poets since medieval times. *Coplas de arte menor*, which include stanzas of *pié quebrado, seguidilla, redondilla, romance*, quatrains, and other brief rhyme schemes, were used particularly as texts for popular vocal and dance music. In the past, both types of *coplas* were used by poets to express religious feelings, love, satire, festive ideas, and political and philosophical thoughts of the common people. Today, the term *coplas* is applied almost exclusively to describe stanzas of popular songs.

The stanza-refrain scheme of the *coplas* movements favors the alternate performance of *coplas* by one or more soloists with the *respuesta* by the vocal ensemble. In setting *coplas* to music, Iribarren explored several possibilities for soloistic performance such as: (a) one soloist for all the *coplas*; (b) a different soloist for each *copla*; (c) *coplas* for duets; (d) one soloist alternating with the other voices; (e) different soloists alternating with the other voices. Of the thirty-five examples examined, only two had the last *copla* of a set scored for the full vocal ensemble.

The overall textual and musical structure of Iribarren's *coplas* is as follows:

Text	Music		
A	a	or	a
B	a		a'
C	a		a"
etc.	etc.		etc.

As has been mentioned before, the traditional link between the *estribillo* and the *coplas* was maintained in the later villancico by repeating the refrain of the *estribillo* as a *respuesta* after each *copla* of the *coplas* movement. Two exceptions to this generalized *coplas—respuestas* pattern are found in the villancicos "Oiga Señor mío" and "Ea, Anfiso alegre." In the first example, the *respuesta* has been omitted; in the second, it has been replaced by an arioso.

In most Iribarren villancicos, *respuestas* are the exact textual and musical repetition of the refrain of the *estribillo* or, less often, of a portion of it. *Respuestas* are sometimes expanded by adding either a section borrowed from the *estribillo* to the refrain, or by adding short new stanzas before each repetition of the *respuesta*. In two of the examples, the original music of the refrain was retained but the text was varied or changed. In only one of the *coplas* movements, the music of the *respuesta* was different from that of the *estribillo*'s refrain. An interesting variant to the *coplas-respuestas* pattern appears in the villancico "Ya que el Niño hermoso." The overall structure for the movement is *copla-respuesta-copla*; *copla-respuesta-coplas*.

Iribarren's *respuestas* show the following organizations within the generalized *coplas-respuestas* scheme.

Text	Music		Text	Music
A	a		A	a
A	a	or less commonly	B	a
A	a		C	a
etc.	etc.		etc.	etc.

The beginning of the *respuestas* section is usually indicated by the words *respuestas a las coplas* or answers to the *coplas*, and frequently reinforced by a double bar-line. In the manuscripts in which this is not specified, the repetition of the textual and musical material makes it obvious. Occasionally, there is a change in meter and/or tempo at the beginning of the *respuestas*. This occurs when the *coplas* are written in a meter and/or tempo different from that of the opening movement in which the material of the *respuesta* has already been established.

Arias:

Francisco Valls, a contemporary of Iribarren, expressed in his book "Mapa armónico practico,"[16] that arias were invented to compensate for the excessive number of recitatives being performed on stage. According to Valls, arias are based on *coplas* of *romances,*[17] *quintillas,*[18] and other lyric verses. In the earlier stage of development, the *copla* of the aria was sung from beginning to end. But at a later date, the *copla* was divided in two parts; the first of which is repeated at the end of the *copla* to conclude the aria. Moreover, Valls asserted that to provide contrast between the parts and make the arias plausible, each part of the *copla* is set to a different mode. In contrast to Valls' simplified statement about the origin of the arias, his description about the form is useful because, to a certain extent, it permits a comparison of Iribarren's compositions with a scheme that was already in existence in Spain.

Arias are included in all of Iribarren's villancicos in three or four movements. In keeping with Valls' description, the sixteen Iribarren arias examined are based either on a two four-line or a two *quintillas* text. The overall ABA tripartite structure of the compositions corresponds to a *da capo* form. The first section of the aria or A section is based on the first four-line or *quintilla* of the text; the second section or B section, on the remainder of the text; the third section is a repetition of the first. The harmonic organization of the three sections as presented below also follows Valls' tonal specifications.

Section A	Section B	Section A
major key	minor key	major key
T—D D—T	R——(D$_r$)	T—D D—T

The A section of the aria consists of two parts which are clearly defined by the repetition of the text and the tonal organization. The first part of the section opens with an instrumental introduction, usually announcing the theme or motives used throughout the aria and preceding the first presentation of the text by one or more soloists. The harmonic progression of this part leads from the tonic to a cadence establishing the dominant key. The repetition of the text in the second

---

[16] Tello, *Teoría Española de la Música,* p. 574.

[17] A genuine Spanish poetic composition characterized by the assonant rhyme of the even lines of the stanza.

[18] Stanza of five isosyllabic verses. Two *quintillas* in a row can be considered a *décima* or ten-line stanza, also called a double *quintilla*. *Quintillas* with or without the same rhyming organization can be freely combined in a poem.

65

part of the A section is also preceded by an instrumental passage which has the dual role of separating the two presentations of the same text and confirming the new key. The harmonic progression of this part leads from the dominant key back to the tonic. The section closes with the complete or partial repetition of the instrumental introduction of the section.

The following scheme shows the formal inner structure of the A section and the only two arrangements of the thematic material found in the sixteen examples of Iribarren's arias.

Text			Music	
————	a	a	instrumental	T
A	a′	b	vocal	T—D
————	a″ or	c	instrumental	D
A	a‴	b′	vocal	D—T
————	a	a	instrumental	T

The B section of the aria is shorter than the A section. It lacks instrumental passages and the text is presented only once. In most arias, a fermata over a diminished or dominant seventh chord is placed at the conclusion of the text, stopping the motion toward the final cadence. After this emphatic preparatory pause, the final cadence is released at a slower tempo. The last cadential measures of the section are sung to the repetition of the last line of the text without instrumental accompaniment. The section ends on the tonic or on the dominant of the relative key. The return to the first section is sometimes marked *D.C.* or *Da Capo.*

The B section as a rule uses the same musical material employed in the vocal parts of the A section. In one of the arias examined, from the villancico "Oh! que halagueña canción," the thematic material, meter and tempo of the second section are different from those of the first section. Exclusive of this example, the two standard structures of the B section are as follows:

Text		Music	
B	a″″ or b″	vocal	R————(D_r)

Arias, by and large, were written in a more learned style than *estribillos* and *coplas.* Developmental devices used by Iribarren in these compositions, and particularly in the second part of the first section, include motives in chromatic progressions, extended vocalizations of sequential passages and occasional phrases of prolonged syncopated lines. Therefore, it is of special interest to point out the aria *juguete*[19] from the villancico "Un juguete mi Niño." The popular character of this aria is brought forth by the quality of the text, simple harmonizations, pedal points of single notes, and intervals of perfect fifths. It is further characterized by rhythms imitative of drum patterns carried by the

---

[19] Refers here to the humorous character of the composition.

continuo, and by the prevalence of a single rhythmic pattern in the instrumental and vocal lines.

Recitatives:

Recitatives and arias are the backbone of Iribarren's villancicos in three, four, and five movements. They are included in the order of recitative and aria in the three- and four-movement villancicos, and in the five-movement villancicos, in the order of recitative, aria, and recitative.

Iribarren's recitatives are short compositions ranging from five to twenty measures. They are usually set to hendecasyllabic verses which are the longest simple verses used in Spanish poetry. This preference for lengthy versification may indicate an approach to a prose-like effect or a pursuit of a contrasting type of versification in relation to the other movements of the villancico.

Of the twenty-three recitative movements examined, nineteen are scored for vocal parts and continuo, and four are for vocal parts with instrumental accompaniment. The nineteen recitatives with only continuo accompaniment are scored as follows:

9	for soprano, alto, and tenor soloists
7	for two sopranos, soprano and alto, soprano and tenor, and alto and tenor
1	for two sopranos, alto, and tenor ensemble
1	for soprano and four-part chorus
1	for two choruses

The four remaining recitatives are scored for the following vocal and instrumental ensembles:

3	for two sopranos, alto, and tenor with violins and continuo accompaniment
1	for two sopranos, alto, tenor, and four-part chorus with oboes, violins, trompas, and continuo accompaniment

A variety of structural procedures is found in Iribarren's recitatives. In the compositions scored for one soloist and continuo, the vocal line progresses either stepwise or in a rather strict chordal motion. The continuo line is always written in long note values. All of these recitatives finish with the quick stereotyped V—I cadence. At the cadence, the vocal line often ends on the dominant followed by the resolving tonic which is played only by the continuo instrument.

Concerning the practices of playing the continuo part to accompany this type of recitative, José de Torres y Martínez Bravo wrote in 1702:

...Se ha de acompañar sin compás, observando por donde camina la voz para dar consonancia al tiempo preciso y en el paraje que le corresponda, por cuya causa se escribe en los acompañamientos que toca. Como también para detenerse o caminar si la voz se detuviera o caminase, para expresar algun afecto, el acompañamiento le espere y le siga.[20]

...It should be freely accompanied but should observe the movement of the vocal line so that consonances are played precisely on time and at the corresponding place; for this purpose the vocal line is written down on the score. If the vocalist should pause to express some kind of affect, the accompanist should also stop and play only when the vocalist continues.

In the composition of recitatives for duets and continuo, Iribarren uses three different techniques: (1) each soloist sings the phrases of the text in alternation; (2) one of the soloists has the responsibility for most of the text; (3) both soloists sing the text simultaneously, either in free intervallic relationship or in strict parallel thirds and sixths.

In the recitatives available for larger vocal ensembles and continuo, Iribarren uses a homorhythmic technique. In both compositions, all the voices simultaneously sing the same text and move at the same rhythm. The continuo accompaniment follows the exact rhythmic progression of the vocal parts.

A similar homorhythmic technique is used in the recitatives with instrumental accompaniment. In these compositions, the vocal and the instrumental ensembles each have their own rhythmic progression. Hence, the rhythmic simultaneity of all the vocal and instrumental parts within each ensemble results in a composition with two homorhythmic progressions.

Iribarren is equally at ease working with vocal lines in a speech-like or melodic style as with his treatment of larger vocal and instrumental ensembles in a measured *accompagnato* style. Whichever style he chooses, he usually maintains it throughout the composition; a choice perhaps justified by the modest size of many of his recitatives. In only a few recitatives for two and three soloists and continuo does Iribarren juxtapose *secco* and arioso passages.

In Iribarren's villancicos, recitatives are always written in a key different from that of the preceding movement. The new key conveys no impression of permanence, since the opening I_6 chord played by the continuo moves immediately into a succession of seventh chords and their inversions. This modulatory progression always leads to a final cadence which establishes the key of the following movement, not the key indicated by the key signature of the recitatives.

The harmonic flexibility of recitatives, in addition to the narrative or dramatic aspect of the text and the freedom of form, point to a dual function of these movements within the villancico structure. They serve as harmonic and textual transitions between movements, as well as a contrast and balance to the recognizable formal and tonal scheme of other movements, particularly to those of the arias.

---

[20] *Reglas de acompañar en organo, clavicordi, y harpa* ("n.p."), p. 98.

Iribarren also incorporated recitative passages in some of the opening movements of his villancicos. Of special interest is the insertion of a recitative *burlesco* in the *estribillo* movement of "Hacer quiere Gil una comedia." The use of this recitative *burlesco* exemplifies the adaptation of secular forms for religious purposes; a musical practice which was highly controversial during several decades of the eighteenth century.

Eustaquio Cerbellon de la Vera, who favored the use of recitatives and other secular forms in the church, asserted that joy and sadness can exist in the church as well as in the theater. In his opinion, the recitative, which depends on the text for its affective expression, could be adapted to both situations.[21]

Iribarren's villancicos in two movements always close with a *coplas* movement, and the villancicos in three movements close with either a *coplas* or an aria movement. However, the closing compositions for the villancicos in four and five movements are variable. In the forty-seven examples selected, these movements are designated as *pastorela, final,* gigue, allegro, and *canción.*

Pastorela:

Generalities about the *pastorela* have already been presented, as Iribarren has included them in opening movements and also in aria movements. Used as a closing movement, the *pastorela* is a through-composed song.

Text		Music
—	a	instrumental
A	b	
B	c	
—	a'	instrumental
C	d	

Finales:

The two *finales* included in the four movements villancicos are short through-composed compositions in a lively 4/4 time. The two textual strophes are set to a symmetrical binary scheme.

Text	Music
A	a
B	b

The *finale* allegro included in a five-movement villancico is an ABA form. Each of the sections is introduced by instrumental measures anticipating the vocal material.

---

[21] *Diálogo armónico sobre el Teatro crítico universal en defensa de la Música de los templos dedicado a las tres capillas reales de esta Corte las de su Majestad, señoras Descalzas y señoras de la Ercanación* (n.p., 1726) pp. 25 and 29.

Gigue:

It is interesting to point out that baroque dance forms were adapted as vocal compositions and were included in the villancico form. One of these forms, the gigue, is the closing movement of a five-movement villancico. Another closing movement, designated as *final airoso*, is also a gigue. These two compositions were written in the same year and included in villancicos *de Calenda*, one for Immaculate Conception Day and the other for Christmas. Both present the same binary formal structure. The compositions are in 6/8 time and have similar rhythmic patterns. Sections A and B are introduced by instrumental passages. Although both villancicos are scored for two choruses, only the first chorus is used in these movements. The movement designated as *final airoso* progresses from the minor to the relative major key; the gigue progresses from the tonic to the dominant. Both movements have elaborate writing for the continuo and violin parts.

Allegro:

Of the two compositions called allegro, one is a two-stanza through-composed composition, and the other consists of only one stanza set to music.

Text	Music	Text	Music
A	a	A	a
B	b		
B'	b' short coda		

Canción:

This strophic movement is in 3/8 time and is scored for two choruses and violins. The text of the two *coplas* consists of three heptasyllabic verses and one pentasyllabic verse. Each *copla* is repeated twice. The first presentation of the *coplas* is by a soloist, and the repetition is based on the same melody, simply harmonized by both choruses. Thus, the textual and musical structure of this canción is as follows:

Text	Music
A	a
A	a'
B	a
B	a'

After examining all of Iribarren's villancicos, and comparing the component movements, it becomes apparent that these compositions can be organized in certain distinct categories. The composer entitled some of his villancicos as *cantadas*, and also suggested certain classifications when he designated some of his works as follows:

Villancicos de   *jácara*
                pastorella
                tonada
                tonadilla
                negros or *negrillos*
                Vizcaíno
                Portugués
                Siciliano
                Calenda

The *cantada* is not different in structure or purpose from those compositions with recitatives and arias which Iribarren entitled "villancicos." The only distinction is that *cantadas* are villancicos scored for one or two soloists, generally with light instrumental accompaniment. This classification, therefore, is termed by the number of its vocal parts.

Jácaras, pastorelas, tonadas, and *tonadillos* are based on specific poetic forms. By designating his villancicos as such, Irribarren implies the inclusion of these musical-poetic forms in his compositions.

The third category indicates the use of dialects and foreign languages in the text of the villancicos. This category includes villancicos *de negros, Vizcaíno, Portugués* and *Siciliano.* It is interesting to point out that in the texts of the villancicos *de negros,* the spelling of the Spanish words is modified to imitate certain peculiarities of speech attributed to the Blacks of Latin-America. For instance, "l" is used in the place of "r;" Francisca, therefore, would be pronounced Flancisca.

Villancicos *de Calenda* and villancicos *de Reyes* are categorized not by poetic form of linguistic usage, but according to the occasions for which they were performed. The *Calenda* was the first, or opening villancico of a set. The latter compositions were performed for the Feast of Epiphany. Although a system of categorization suggested by Iribarren's manuscripts' titles is functional, it is also limited in the sense that an overlapping of categories could possibly occur.

A fundamental feature of the villancico as a genre is the amalgamation of varient compositions derived from Spanish musical and lyrical sources and from foreign influences. It is felt that a classification based on the combination of these component movements would present a more revealing overview of the development of the villancico form in the eighteenth century.

According to these criteria, three types of villancicos have emerged:

Type I consists of those villancicos in two movements which retain the traditional Spanish musical-poetic forms such as the *estribillo*-like and *coplas* movements.

71

Type II consists of villancicos in three or more movements which use recitatives, arias, and other baroque forms, excluding the Spanish forms.

Type III, a "hybrid" type, consists of those villancicos in three or more movements which combine the Spanish elements with other musical forms.

These three types of villancicos were performed for all major Church festivities. Because of the diversity of subject matter and musical compositions offered by these various structural types, the villancico suited the well educated as well as the less knowledgeable members of the congregation. The association of music and secular poetry in the villancico played an important role in the communication between the Church and the Spanish people.

The more expanded villancicos, those which included recitatives and arias, were usually performed as opening villancicos in the various festivities. These compositions, called *Calendas*, were usually set to an erudite text, and scored for large vocal and instrumental ensembles. The poetry used for these villancicos made use of metaphors and other complex poetic structures, in accordance with the more serious nature of the occasion. Performance of villancicos with recitatives and arias also seemed to have prevailed on Immaculate Conception Day.

Villancicos in two or more movements, containing traditional Peninsular material, were performed particularly at Christmas and are by far the most abundant of those available at the Malaga cathedral. As the most joyous holiday of the liturgical calendar, Christmas lent itself to the use of texts and music reflecting the pleasures and happiness of simple life.

The use of recitatives and arias and other secular forms within the Church was a matter of great controversy during the seventeenth and eighteenth centuries. Iribarren rose above these much criticized abuses, demonstrating an ability to temper the musical excesses of the Italian style and to elevate popular Spanish musical forms to a level appropriate to the solemnity of the divine service.

CHAPTER VII

FIVE VILLANCICOS BY JUAN FRANCÉS DE IRIBARREN

Analysis of Compositional Devices

All of the Iribarren manuscripts consulted for this research are preserved in the Music Library of the Malaga Cathedral. Although instrumental and vocal parts were available for most of the villancicos, full scores have been the primary sources for this study. Full scores and parts bear only the name of the composer. If some of them are transcribed by copyists, as some of the notation and handwriting seems to indicate, the copyists have not been identified.

To convey a better understanding of Iribarren's work in this genre, five of the forty-seven compositions originally selected for this research have been transcribed in this volume. The five villancicos transcribed are "A Belén caminad pastorcillos," "A Belén, a Belén pastorcillas," "Las zagalas de Belén," "Alados celestiales," and "Aves acordes." As a description of the overall structure and an analysis of the component movements have been offered in Chapter VI, only an analysis of Iribarren's compositional procedures will be presented here. Problems of transcription of the five selected villancicos will also be discussed.

These five villancicos are representative of the classification of Iribarren's villancicos suggested in the previous chapter. They were basically selected according to the type of compositions used for the various movements. However, in making the selection, the number of vocal parts, instrumentation, occasion of performance, and compositional procedures were also considered.

The number of vocal parts of these villancicos range from two to eight. Iribarren's techniques of vocal writing are summarized in the writing of Francisco Valls, who expressed that extremes of vocal range should not be overused; that two vocal lines should move in intervalic relationship of thirds and sixths; that the writing for three voices needs more imitation; and that the voices of a four-part choir should be treated as soloistics.[1]

Nasarre emphasizes that in Spain, the vocal lines in compositions for more than four parts still maintain their independence, unlike in other countries, in which the lines of the second choir usually double the lines of the first.[2] Iribarren always gives variety to the vocal ensembles by exchanging the roles of the vocal lines. In working with the standard vocal quartet, he often assigns the melodic lines to two of the parts, and the other two parts act as supportive harmony. In compositions for eight or more voices, according to Andres Lorente, choirs should sing in alternation and imitation; vocal lines of each choir should be presented independently; and simultaneous singing advisable

---

[1]   *Mapa armónico-práctico.* Cited in Tello, *La Teoría Española*, pp. 569-71.
[2]   *Escuela Música*, 2: 36-37.

at cadential points.[3] This choir treatment is found in all Iribarren villancicos.

The composer also agrees with Nasarre, who asserts that compositions for five and six vocal parts are usually treated as compositions for a soloist or duet with choral accompaniment.[4] In support of Nasarre, Francisco Valls adds that the soloist of the duet in the compositions in five or six vocal lines act as the concertino in the concerto grosso.[5]

The compositional procedures followed by Iribarren in the use of voices combined with instruments agree with the writings of his contemporary Valls who asserted that violins generally support the soprano line; that violins can accompany the vocal lines in unison; that the compositions for soloists, violin, oboes, and flutes blend harmoniously because these instruments can imitate the human voice and play the same melodies.[6] Of interest is Valls' advice for larger instrumental ensembles in combination with a small vocal ensemble. He recommends avoidance of presenting both ensembles together. It is preferable to present the two elements separately, and later in combination.[7] This procedure, as a rule, is found in most of Iribarren's compositions with that type of score.

Iribarren, in general, used a comfortable range for the instrumentation. However, the *trompas* are often used to the extreme of the lower register. The demands in range for violins, oboes, and flutes are similar. Oboes and violins usually play the same melody, although oboes in such combination can have a soloistic role. The flute usually plays in a register higher than the oboe.

All Iribarren's villancicos are performed with a continuo instrument. The amount of figures in the thoroughbass depends usually on the type of composition. Because of the simpler harmonic nature of the villancicos of popular character, there is less figured bass indications in them than in those containing recitatives and arias. The organ and occasionally the harp are used in Iribarren's villancicos as continuo instruments. Pizzicato and *con arco* imply indications in the continuo line of the use of a string instrument. This unidentified instrument could be a string bass.

Iribarren does not rely excessively in word-painting; nevertheless, he uses this device particularly in opening movements to convey meanings of subjective words and phrases or to interpret sounds of nature, objects, or instrumental effects. Some of the word-painting uses from this period are described by Valls. Emotions and ideas in high register:

---

[3] *El porque de la música*, (Alcalá de Henares: Imprenta de Nicolás de Xamares, 1762), p. 520.

[4] *Escuela Música*, 2: 321.

[5] *Mapa armónico-práctico*. Cited in Tello, *La Teoría Española,* pp. 569-71.

[6] *Ibid.*, p. 566.

[7] *Ibid.*, p. 565.

happiness
festiveness
elements of air
fire
sky
mountains

Emotions and ideas in high register and with dotted rhythms:

arrogance
presumptuousness
desperation

Emotions and ideas in lower register:

sadness
pain
earth
water
darkness
valleys
the abyss.

Expressions of admiration contain pauses in the music; humiliation is in a slow tempo.

The movements of Iribarren's villancicos are written in keys with no more of three sharps or three flats in the key signature. Minor keys usually do not show the actual key signatures. The minor modes even at the time of Padre Soler were explained by the octave of the "re" mode or first authentic mode. According to the hexachordal system, the mode consisted of two consecutive intervals of fourths: re, mi, fa, sol, and re, mi, fa, sol. Therefore, according to this structure the c minor scale appears with only two flats in the key signature and the b minor with three sharps.[8]

Padre Soler's book, published in 1762, coincides with the end of Iribarren's career as a composer, but reflects some of the current practice of the time. In regard to modulation, Soler advises the use of chords common to both tonalities. He emphasizes the function of the dominant chord, but distinguishes between "fast" modulation and prolonged modulatory passages in which the melody progresses through other keys before reaching the final one.[9] This latter modulation is particularly used by Iribarren in recitatives and in the second section of most arias.

---

[8] *Llave de modulación y antiguedades de la música,* (Madrid: Taller de Joaquín Ibarra, 1762), pp. 72-75.

[9] *Ibid.,* p. 81.

In the transcription of unpublished historical scores, it is of paramount importance to convey the composer's intention as accurately as possible. However, in preparing the scores of Iribarren's villancicos, some changes were introduced to facilitate the study of the works and to conform with the modifications in notational and performing practices since Iribarren's time.

The title page of each manuscript has been reproduced on the title page of the transcription. However, as the original settings of the text are provided with the analysis of the works, the words which are abbreviated in the original have been written in full in the transcription. The information included at the top of the first page of the score, referring to the composer, date, and occasion of performance, has been retained. The instrumentation, however, has been deleted as that information is specified in the musical score itself.

The manuscripts convey, in general, the composer's intention. Measures encompassing the full score are clearly delineated by bar lines which have been drawn free-handed. Often, the number of beats in each measure is twice as large as the number of beats indicated in the time signatures and occasionally two measures have been barred together. Note values in the instrumental parts are grouped in metrical units which conform with present day notational practices, although the rhythmic groups do not always adjust in the vertical alignment with those of other staves. Pitches are indicated by a precise positioning of the notes on the staff. In instances in which notes have been erased and rewritten, the syllable names corresponding to the hexachordal system are found close to the notes corrected, in order to avoid confusion.

For the scoring of the vocal parts, Iribarren used the clefs, which were in common practice in his time. In the vocal transcription, however, the treble clef has been used for the soprano and alto parts, and also for the tenor with the numeral "8" attached to the bottom of the clef indicating that the part should be sung one octave lower than written.

In the full scores, all instruments are written in concert pitch. With the exception of the *trompas*, which in addition to the treble clef are written with the soprano, mezzo-soprano, tenor, and bass clef in the third line, and the *bajoncillos*, which are written with the soprano clef, all instruments are written with treble clefs. *Trompas* have been transcribed with treble and bass clefs.

Various sources define the trompa as similar to the French horn, or as an instrument akin to the modern trumpet. Francisco Valls differentiates between the old *trompa* and the one in use during the eighteenth century. He does not describe the instrument, but states that the old *trompa* was on F and the range extended from f below the bass clef to f below the treble clef, and the modern was in D with the range extending from d below the treble clef to d two ledger lines above the staff.[10] However, in Iribarren's full scores which were examined, the

---

[10] *Mapa armónico-poetico.* Cited in Tello, *La Teoría Española,* pp. 564-66.

writing applies to the *trompas* in C. The range assigned to the *trompas* permits performing of these parts by either C or B♭ modern trumpets or by a French horn. Therefore, the transcription has not specified any of these instruments, leaving the designation for *trompas* as written in the original. The other instrument used in Iribarren's villancicos is the clarín. It has been described by Nasarre as similar to the *trompas* but smaller and of a higher pitch,[11] and by Tomás Vicente Tosca, in the seventeenth century, as an instrument of greater length.[12]

Iribarren's notational practices are very similar to the notation in common use. Yet, some peculiarities are consistently found in his manuscripts. The differences encountered in the writing of note values, as the examples below show, are: (a) a downward stem always placed to the right side of the note; (b) a sixteenth note by itself written as an eighth note with a diagonal stroke through the flag; (c) a thirty-second note by itself written as the sixteenth note described above with a stroke through the stem; (d) a large note value occasionally written directly on the bar line instead of two equivalent small note values tied across the bar line.

Rests vary in their placement on the staff. A rest is usually written on the line or space nearest to the note that follows it. Rest values are notated as follows:

One measure of rest is notated by an equivalent rest value generally accompanied by the numeral "1." More than one measure of rest is consistently written in the following way: instead of assigning a rest for each individual measure, the measures are left blank and the total number is indicated in the last measure by a numeral and the corresponding rest symbols. Below are examples of measures as they appeared in the manuscripts. The position of the rest symbols changes after each multiple of eight has been reached.

At times, instrumental or vocal parts which sound in unison, are not written down, but are only indicated as such. For clarity, these measures have been copied down in the transcription.

Iribarren's compositions have several indications of tempo, dynamics, articulation and texture.

[11] *Escuela Música*, 1:480.
[12] Tello, *La Teoría Española*, pp. 62-64.

Tempo marks are:

> grave
> adagio
> andante
> moderato
> allegro moderato
> *algo sosegado*
> *amoroso* (with emotion)
> *a medio aire* (Alla breve)
> *algo airioso* (somewhat arioso)
> arioso (arioso)
> spiritoso
> allegro
> allegro gustoso
> allegro assai
> *vivo*
> *quedo* (slower)

Dynamic indications are:

> Po. (piano)
> fe. (fuerte)
> *suabe* (soft)
> *eco*
> *con sordina*

Texture is indicated by:

> tutti
> solo
> duo
> unísono
> tacet
> tasto solo

The following designation for articulation:

> *punteado*
> pizzicato
> *arco*

Ornamentations found in Iribarren's score are as follows:

Referring to the manner in which some of the ornaments should be played, Nasarre, speaking about the keyboard instruments, describes the trill as having a minimum of five notes which should be played with the third and fourth fingers of the right hand, or with the thumb and the index of the left hand. He recommends to also practice these trills with other fingers. He emphasizes that in Spanish music, trills, unlike Bach trills, should be played starting on the notes. Another ornament, the mordent, or *aleo* or *aleado*, consists of only three notes, either ascending or descending.[13]

Very few changes have been made in the transcription of Iribarren's villancicos. Some refer to the grouping of note values to facilitate the reading, or rewriting the notes when ties over the bar line were necessary. Changes which have been made in the transcription have been indicated in brackets.

Analytical Overview of the Five Transcriptions

1.   A Belén Caminad Pastorcillos

This villancico entitled *cantada* is one of the earliest works of Juan Francés de Iribarren and it was the third villancico performed during the Christmas celebration of 1736. The manuscript consists of nine and one-half unnumbered pages of music of 12.4 x 8.4 inches. On the cover page the composition is identified as "Villan.co 3o/Cantada a duo con V.V.s/ al Nacim.to del nño Redemp.or/A Belén Caminad Pastorcillos/del Mro. dn.Ju. francs de Iribarrn/Año 1736." On the first page of the score similar information is repeated: "Cantada a Duo al sto Nacim.to con VVs. del Mro. Iribarren Año 1736."

The *cantada* consists of five movements: Introduction, Recitative, Aria, Recitative, and *Pastorela*. It is scored for two soloists, alto and tenor, with continuo and two violin parts.

The introduction in G major corresponds to a brief seventeen-measure ABA form. It is unified by the rhythmic pattern

which is used in alternation by voices and violins. It is a very compact form with a modulation to the dominant key in the B section. The vocal lines move in parallel thirds and sixths and they only attain a certain melodic independence at cadential points.

The first recitative is scored for soprano and continuo. It starts with an I6 chord in C major and progresses somewhat chromatically to establish the e minor tonality of the aria.

The aria has the overall brief *da capo* structure discussed in the aria section of Chapter VI, and it is scored for two soloists and continuo. The most striking feature of this aria is that there is no idiomatic difference between the treatment of the violin and vocal parts. Almost every syllable of the text is sung to two or more notes. Unlike the cadential vocal formulas of the introductory movement, the vocal parts in the aria are sung in parallel intervals of thirds only in the modulatory

---

[13] *Escuela Música*, 2: 470-71.

passages. Cadential points, although sung in parallel motion, are heavily ornamented.

The second recitative is scored for two soloists and continuo. It begins on a C major sixth chord and progresses to G major in a succession of dominant and diminished seventh chords. The soloists after singing the two first phrases of the text in alternation, continue to move in parallel thirds until the final cadence.

A *pastorela* in G major constitutes the closing movement. This movement is a through-composed song. The first two strophes of the composition are introduced by an instrumental passage which is repeated before the third strophe. In contrast to the introduction and the aria movements, which were rhythmically complex and used many contrapuntal compositional devices, this *pastorela* is simply harmonized. The interest lies in the long tonal phrases and in the repetition of certain motives reminiscent of dance rhythms. The return to G major seems to be the only element preserving the unity of the form. Every movement has its own entity and does not share musical materials with the other movements.

2.   A Belén, A Belén Pastorcillas

In this composition we shall see that Iribarren combines the elements of traditional Spanish music with the compositional techniques of the art music tradition. The manuscript is identified on the first page of the score as "Villan.co de Navidad de tonadilla a 7, con Violon.s y trompas./Del Mro. Iribarren Año 1749." It is indicated on the last page that it was performed as the third villancico during the Christmas celebration.

This two-movement villancico is based on the traditional *estribillo-coplas* scheme. Both movements are scored for two choirs, first and second violin, and first and second *trompa*. The vocal arrangement for the first choir is soprano, alto and tenor; the second choir has the standard soprano, alto, tenor, and bass arrangement.

The *estribillo* movement is an expanded *estribillo* including an introductory stanza and a *tonadilla* section. The first two lines of the introductory stanza are sung by the first and second choirs in alternation. The overlapping imitation by the choirs in the remaining four lines of the stanza produces an accelerando effect, balanced however by the melodic lines of the violins, which play the vocal melody in augmentation. The role of the continuo and the *trompas* in this introduction is only of harmonic support. In the *estribillo* per se, the soloist, a shepherdess, asks friends if they have seen Bato, the keeper of the herd. The choir responds that Bato is a simple lad who does not accept the Child's help. During this dialogue between the soloist and the choirs, the instrumental accompaniment provides only the supportive harmony while the choir sings, but participates when the soloist performs by imitating the vocal lines.

The *tonadilla* section corresponds to the type of strophic song discussed in the previous chapter. In one *tonadilla* stanza, the soloist asks the Child which winds will bring him to the harbor of this Earth, and advises the Child to stay away from this treacherous harbor. The choirs repeat the soloist's section in unison, although omitting the bass.

The *coplas* movement consists of five *coplas* and five *respuestas*; four of the five *coplas* are sung by the soloists, and the last one by both choirs. The five *respuestas* have different texts and are sung by both choirs to the same music. The music of the *coplas* movement corresponds to the music of the *tonadillas* included in the *estribillo*. The only difference is that in the *coplas* movements the violins and *trompas* participate more actively in the presentation or imitation of the phrases sung by the soloists or choirs.

To keep the simplicity of the popular style, Iribarren has worked only within the frame of G major; the continuo has maintained a drum-like rhythmic pattern almost throughout the composition; the vocal parts are written for the normal range of voices. To balance the simplicity of the melodic line, Iribarren has used contrapuntal techniques of imitation and augmentation.

3.   *Las Zagalas de Belén*

On the first page of music, this composition is identified as "Villancico de tonadilla de Navidad, a 8 con violines y trompas; del Mro. Iribarren, Año 1752." On the last page of the manuscript, it is indicated that this villancico was to be performed sixth. The size of the manuscript is 8.4 x 12.4 inches. The inclusion of a *tonadilla* in the first movement reflects the influence of popular elements. It is scored for a first choir of two sopranos, alto, and tenor, and a second choir of standard vocal arrangement.

The *estribillo* in this villancico shows an overall formal structure similar to the *estribillo* analyzed in "A Belén Pastorcillas." The introductory stanza is sung only by the second choir: two of the vocal parts carry the melody and the other two parts provide harmonic support. While the *trompas* play the fundamental note of the tonic or dominant chords, the violin and continuo have a rapid melodic line. The *estribillo* per se begins with both choirs singing the first line of the stanza in unison. Both choirs sing the remaining lines of the stanza in alternation, overlapping the end of each phrase. This is the same device described in the introduction of "A Belén Pastorcillas." The second stanza is introduced by a soloist, but in the second line of the stanza, in which the word "repitan," or "repeat" appears, the chorus sings the word "repitan" in alternation several times to reinforce the meaning of the word. Both choruses finish the last part of the stanza in unison, and the *estribillo* movement finishes with a repeated I, VI, II, V, I instrumental cadence.

The *coplas* movement is in G major, the same as the *estribillo*. The *coplas* section consists of four *coplas*, set to the same music. The time signature of the section is 6/8, but the measures actually alternate between 3/4 and 6/8 time. The soloist, who is the soprano of the first choir, sings each line of the verse in alternation with the violins and *trompas*. The phrases sung by the soloist consist of one measure of 3/4 time; the alternating instrumental measures are in 6/8 time. This hemiola device is used throughout the *coplas* section. The last two lines of the *coplas* are repeated with the soloist and the violin performing the same material in 6/8 time, and the *trompas* playing simpler material in 3/4 time.

The *respuestas* are sung by the first soprano of the first chorus accompanied by the vocal ensemble. The first three lines of the stanza of the *respuestas* are a dialogue between the soloist and both choirs. It is of interest to point out that the phrase used by the soloist corresponds to a simplified version in 3/4 of the first phrase of the *coplas*. The last verses of the *respuesta*, in which the text refers to the snipping sound made by lamb shears, is sung by both choirs. The violin and the soprano simulate the "bah-ah-ah" of the lamb in five beats of 16 notes, indicated as pizzicato.

The "chas-chas" of the shears is sung by the entire vocal ensemble. The *respuestas* finish with a long instrumental passage.

Iribarren incorporates word-painting in his more sophisticated villancicos as well as using this technique in those villancicos of popular character. In the former type, this device is used to convey subjective meanings. But for those villancicos of more common character, metaphor is seldom used, and onomatopoeic devices refer directly to their counterparts in objects and in nature, with no subtlety intended.

4.   *Alados Celestiales Querubines*

This composition was used as an opening villancico for the feast of the Blessed Sacrament, and was entitled by Iribarren as "Entrada Ayrosa Villan.^co de Kalenda al SS.^mo a 7 con violin.^s oboe tromp.^s y clarin.^s del Mro. Iribarren. 1754."

The full score consists of eight pages, 8-3/8 x 12-3/8 inches, numbered from one to eight. The work is in three movements: *Entrada*, Recitative, and Aria. The score calls for a recorder (flauta dulce), oboe, two *trompas*, two violins, continuo, and two choirs. The first choir consists of soprano, alto, and tenor. The second has the standard vocal arrangement.

Of the forty-seven examples examined, this is the only villancico which has a complete instrumental *entrada*. It is in ABA form, and in the style of a concerto grosso. The A section, in G major, begins with a tutti section which leads to a cadential point on D major. The second part of the A section is entrusted to the concertino, consisting of an oboe which has the responsibility of the melodic line, and two violins providing the supporting harmony. This is a modulatory part which establishes the keys of d minor and a minor through sequential motives based on diminished seventh chords to lead finally to the B section in a D major key. The B section of the *entrada* is very similar to the A section, except the tutti is in the key of D major, and the concertino part brings it back to G major. The last A section is constituted only by the tutti movement. In this particular movement the continuo is excluded from the concertino passages. In general, this manuscript has little indication for the realization of the continuo.

The recitative of this villancico is one of the few examples scored for large vocal and instrumental ensembles. Each one of the first three lines of the recitative text is given respectively to the soprano, alto, and tenor of the first chorus. Each of these lines is separated by an instrumental phrase. The last phrase is sung by the entire vocal ensemble, accompanied by the full instrumental section. In this type of recitative, Iribarren uses a homorhythmic technique for the vocal and instrumental ensembles. These recitatives are less chromatic than those for one or two soloists and continuo. They begin with the stereotyped tonic sixth chord. Unlike the recitative for one or two soloists, in which the vocal line often ends on the dominant, these recitatives' vocal lines have a full final cadence reinforced by the instrumental parts. Still, the feeling of inconclusiveness typical to the vocal lines is transferred to the *trompas*, which suddenly stop on the dominant before the final cadence.

The aria of "Alados Celestiales Querubines" is a lively, driving movement *alla breve*. Both the overall structure and the inner structure of the two sections of Iribarren's arias have been amply discussed in Chapter VI. The aria in this villancico belongs to the monothematic type. Of interest is the concerto grosso-like treatment which has been given to this aria. The concertino part of the instrumental ensemble has been assigned to the oboe, and of the vocal ensemble to the soprano. In the introductory instrumental part of the A section, the theme is presented by the oboe. In the first presentation of the text, the soloist repeats the same materials introduced by the oboe. In this a' part of the A section, the oboe accompanies the vocal line in a canon-like manner. Almost every line of the text begins with the word *"cantad,"* an imperative form of the word "sing." The element of command implied, combined with the elating experience of singing, has been transferred into the musical structure. After each intonation of *"cantad"* sung by the soloist, the entire vocal ensemble, either in alternation or simultaneously, and accompanied by the instrumental ensemble, respond by joyously repeating *"cantad."*

As a monothematic aria, the same treatment of the material continues through. Unlike many of the villancicos of popular character used in these festivities to entertain the congregation, this opening piece, a fine example of a villancico *de Calenda*, serves to uplift the spirit and arouse the religious emotions of the congregation.

5.   *Las Aves Acordes*

This villancico was written in 1756 for the festival of Corpus Christi. The manuscript consists of eight pages 8-3/8 x 12-3/8 inches, numbered from one to eight. The music is written on both sides of each page, except for the last page, which has music on only side. At the top of the first page, the villancico is identified as "Villan.^{co} de Corpus a 8 con violin.^s y oboe del Mro. Iribarr.ⁿ Año 1756."

The work is written in three movements: *Entrada*, Recitative, and Aria. It is scored for recorder (flauta dulce), oboe, two *trompas*, two violins, continuo, and two choruses. The first chorus consists of first and second soprano, alto, and tenor; the second consists of soprano, alto, tenor, and bass.

The *entrada* has two sections indicated as allegro gustoso and moderato. As in the other villancicos *de Calenda* which have been examined, this composition starts with a forceful and rhythmic drive. The movement begins with an instrumental section in which the theme is introduced. The same material is repeated in the vocal parts by the two sopranos of the first choir. The second line of the text, always using the same musical material, is sung by the second choir. When Iribarren works with four vocal parts, the melodic line is often given to two of the vocal lines, and the remaining two are used as supporting harmony. The last line of the first strophe is given to the alto and tenor of the first choir. In the second strophe the process of alternation of the vocal parts is reversed. It starts with the second choir, and the second and third lines of the verse are sung in duet by the two sopranos and by the alto and tenor of the first choir. The last line is sung by both choirs. It could be said that the structural devices of this section are based on the words of the text. The alternation of the vocal parts seems to coincide with the singing of the word "alternen," or "alternate." This also appears to be true for the last verse in which the text expresses the idea of singing together in the phrase "let us sing together."

The text of the second section of the first movement expresses "my beloved is sleeping; my master is sleeping; rest, my life; rest, my heaven." Because of the nature of the text, this section is written in slower tempo than the first. The first two lines of the text are presented in alternation by the first and second choir. The third and fourth lines of the text are also presented by the first and second choir, but each line here is melodically independent. The last line of the text is repeated in very long values by the whole vocal ensemble, giving the feeling of rest. Each presentation of these textual lines is preceded by the syllable *"ce."* The Castilian pronunciation of the letter "c," which places the tongue behind the teeth, suggests that this syllable may have been performed as a sound instead of as a syllable, to reinforce the idea of "sleep" and "rest" in the text. Before each textual line, the choirs repeat the syllable *"ce"* in different rhythmic combinations.

The treatment of the recitative of this villancico is no different from those recitatives already analyzed. It is scored for the soprano and alto of the first choir with continuo accompaniment. The structural pattern of this recitative consists of the alternate singing of the first verses by the soloists and the simultaneous rendition for the last two verses. It is of interest, however, to point out that these vocal lines do not progress in the usual parallel thirds and sixths, but are modulatory melodic lines.

The aria has the same formal structure of the arias analyzed in Chapter VI. Although not indicated in the score as such, this aria has all the characteristics found in compositions called *pastorelas*. It is in 12/8 and the prevalent rhythmic patterns coincide with those of the *pastorela*. However, it demonstrates greater harmonic complexity than the *pastorelas* found in villancicos of a more popular character and the ornamentation and vocalization of syllables, particularly at cadential points, is in keeping with the aria style.

This villancico does not have thematic unity among the movements. This is true even for the two sections of the first movement. The only relation seems to be a key relation. The first movement starts in the key of G major, and the aria is written in the parallel minor key.

Conclusion

The work of Juan Francés de Iribarren has remained largely in manuscript form, and until now there has been no specific study of his music. Although this book has not examined the totality of his musical output, the study of Iribarren's villancicos can convey some understanding of his compositional procedures.

Iribarren's villancicos are vocal religious compositions in two or more movements with instrumental accompaniment, combining elements unique to the Spanish lyric with recitatives, arias, and other baroque forms. His villancicos are scored for one to no more than eight voices. The instrumental ensemble makes use of violins, flutes, oboe, *trompas*, and also of instruments particularly Spanish, such as *chirimías* and *bajones*. Iribarren's idiom is a blend of harmonic vocabulary with contrapuntal techniques.

The movements in Iribarren's villancicos are usually written in different keys which are not always closely related, and do not often share thematic musical materials, and sometimes not even textual material. Only the *estribillo*-like and the *coplas* movements are closely bound. That is, when both movements are included in the same villancico, regardless of the number of movements, they are bound by the refrain of the *estribillo*-like movements, which is almost always repeated in the *respuestas* section of the *coplas* movement. Recitatives could be considered, to a certain extent, to function as connective movements, serving as a modulatory vehicle between movements in different keys.

Villancicos have often been referred to as Spanish cantatas because of the inclusion of recitatives and arias. This terminology is not all-inclusive because there are many villancicos which do not use these forms at all. Iribarren has entitled some of his compositions *cantadas*; although they include recitatives and arias, they are not different in overall structure from those compositions called villancicos which also include recitatives and arias. In Iribarren's examples, the difference refers to the limitation to one or two soloists in the *cantadas*.

Many Iribarren villancicos are designated as *de jácara, de seguidilla, de negros, pastorela*, etc. This does not refer to the use of specific musical structures, but to poetic forms, stereotyped characters or subject matters peculiar to Spain and its colonies. However, there are some definite associations between the musical and non-musical elements, resulting in characteristics unique to these compositions.

Juan Francés de Iribarren is practically an unknown composer, and only a handful of his compositions have been published in scholarly collections of baroque music. Through his villancicos, Iribarren demonstrates an understanding of the musical forms of his time, as well as command of the compositional devices of art music. He is a skillful craftsman, and although his compositions follow already established structural patterns, within those patterns he achieves variety. He does not favor the dramatic and ornamental excesses to which many composers of his period were addicted. Similarly, Iribarren never succumbed to the easy satire and roguishness of the popular text, or to the highly elaborate style of baroque poetry.

Iribarren's talent lies in his understanding and familiarity with the work of his contemporaries, and in his ability to integrate the techniques of learned music with popular elements of Spanish forms of dance and songs. His music is representative of the religious musical trends of his time. Its performance could awaken interest not only in Iribarren's work, but in the music of other composers of this period, who have been all but forgotten. The furthering of knowledge of the villancico will bring a better understanding not only of this form, but of the musical heritage of Spain in the eighteenth century.

APPENDICES

APPENDIX A

CHRONOLOGICAL LIST OF MALAGA
CATHEDRAL CHAPELMASTERS UP TO 1803[1]

Hernán Lopez	1513-19
Diego Fernandez (or Hernandez)	1519-51
Cristobal de Morales	1551-53
Francisco Guerrero	1554 (resigned before taking possession of his job)
Juan Cepa	1554-76
Pedro Periañez	1578-83
Francisco Carrillo	1584-85
Francisco Vasquez	1586-1612
Esteban Brito	1613-40
Juán Perez Roldan	1642-45
Francisco Ruiz Samaniego	1646-54
Francisco Navarro (substitute)	1655-60
Francisco Ruiz Samaniego	1660-66
Juán Montañez (substitute)	1666
Alonso Torices	1666-83
Francisco Sanz	1684-1732
Manuel Martinez Delgado	1732 (died before taking possession of his job)
Juán Francés de Iribarren	1733-67
Jaime Torrens	1770-1803

---

[1] Andrés Llordén, "Notas historicas de los maestros de capilla en la Catedral de Malaga." *Anuario Musical* 20 (1967): 160.

APPENDIX B

INVENTORY OF THE WORKS OF JUAN FRANCÉS DE IRIBARREN AS CATALOGUED IN THE MUSIC LIBRARY OF THE MALAGA CATHEDRAL[1]

Legajo		*Compositions*
I	Villancicos and motets	1-20
II	Villancicos, motets and one cantata	21-37
III	Collection of "Regina caeli" and Christmas villancicos	38-58
IV	Collection of "Regina caeli" and Christmas villancicos	59-78
V	*Salve Regina* motets for the Blessed Virgin Mary	79-88
VI	Cantatas, arias and villancicos	89-118
VII	Psalms, motets and villancicos	119-44
VIII	Invitatories and Christmas villancicos	145-52
IX	Motets for the Blessed Virgin Mary	153-76
X	Cantatas and duets for the Blessed Sacrament	177-200
XI	Villancicos and cantatas for the Blessed Sacrament, and Christmas villancicos	201-30
XII	Villancicos and cantatas for the Blessed Sacrament, and Christmas villancicos	231-46

---

[1] Iribarren compositions are organized in forty-one *legajos*. From *legajo* I through XX, the compositions are consecutively numbered throughout. The twenty-four remaining *legajos* are not sequentially numbered, but the compositions themselves are consecutively numbered beginning with "one" in each *legajo*.

APPENDIX C

"THE 1770 MUSIC INVENTORY OF THE MALAGA CATHEDRAL"[1]

Works in Latin

Masses with and without instruments

1. 7 voices, with instruments
2. 7 voices
3. 8 voices
4. 4 voices
5. 4 voices
6. 4 voices
7. 4 voices
8. 5 voices
9. 4 voices
10. 4 voices
11. A duet
12. 8 voices, without instruments, based on the *Cantate Domino*
13. 5 voices, with instruments
14. 4 voices, with organ continuo
15. 5 voices, without instruments, based on the hymn, Caelestis Urbes
16. 2 choruses
17. 2 choruses
18. 4 voices, with solo voice, duplicated in the second choir, without instruments

Misereres with instruments

1. 6 voices
2. 6 voices
3. 6 voices
4. 6 voices
5. 6 voices
6. 6 voices
7. 6 voices
8. 6 voices
9. 6 voices
10. 8 voices
11. 8 voices
12. 4 voices, duplicated
13. 8 voices
14. 8 voices
15. 8 voices

---

[1] Translation of the "Inventario Musical de 1770" found by Father Andrés Llordén in the archives of the Malaga Cathedral and published in *Anuario Musical* 24 (1970): 237-246.

16. 8 voices
17. 8 voices
18. 8 voices
19 8 voices
    4 voices
20. 8 voices
21. 8 voices
22. 3 separate choruses

Lamentations for Wednesday of Holy Week with choruses and soloists with instruments

1. 7 voices, first
2. 8 voices, first
    7 voices, first, for Maundy Thursday
3. 7 voices, for Wednesday
4. solo, second
5. solo, second
6. solo, second
7. solo, second
8. solo, third
9. solo, third
10. solo, third

Lamentations for choir and soloists for Maundy Thursday

11. 7 voices, first
12. solo, second
13. solo, second
14. solo, second
15. solo, third
16. solo, third
17. solo, third

Lamentations for soloists for Good Friday

18. solo, second
19. solo, second
20. solo, second
21. solo, third, the Lamentation of Jeremias

Sequences with instruments

1. 8 voices, for the Holy Spirit
2. 8 voices, for the Resurrection
3. 5 voices, for the Blessed Sacrament

Sequences without instruments

5. solo, for the Resurrection

8. 5 voices, for the sorrows of the Blessed Virgin Mary
9. 5 voices, for the sorrows of the Blessed Virgin Mary
10. 5 voices, for the sorrows of the Blessed Virgin Mary
11. 8 voices, for the Blessed Sacrament
12. 2 choruses, for the Blessed Sacrament
13 solo, for the Blessed Sacrament
14. 5 voices, for the Holy Spirit
15. solo, for the Holy Spirit

Vespers with instruments for the Blessed Virgin Mary

1. 8 voices, one set
2. 6 voices
3. 7 voices
4. 6 voices

For Our Lord and Saints

6. 8 voices
7. 6 voices
8. 7 voices
9. 8 voices
10. 6 voices, for Corpus Christi

Complines

1. 8 voices, one set without instruments
2. 5 voices, with violins
3. 6 voices, with violins
4. 6 voices, with violins

Te Deum Laudamus with instruments

1. 8 voices
2. 7 voices

Vexilla Regis

1. 8 voices
2. 7 voices

Hymns for Corpus Christi

1. 4 voices, *Pange lingua*

Office of the Dead, with and without instruments

1. 8 voices, Office for the Dead
2. 4 voices, Office for the Dead
3. 7 voices, Mass

4. 6 voices, Lesson *Parce mihi*
5.   solo, motet
6. 8 voices, motet, with instruments
7. 3 voices, motet
8. 8 voices, Lesson *Parce mihi*, without instruments
9. 8 voices, motet and responsory, without instruments
10.   solo, motet and responsory
11. 8 voices, lesson *Parce mihi*

Invitatories to the Birth of Our Lord

1. 8 voices, without instruments
2. 6 voices, with instruments
3. 8 voices, with instruments
4. 8 voices, with instruments
5. 7 voices, with instruments

Salves for the Blessed Virgin Mary with and without instruments

1. 5 voices, with instruments
2. 6 voices
3. 6 voices
4. 7 voices
5. 8 voices
6. 4 voices
7. 4 voices
8. 4 voices
9. 4 voices
10. 4 voices
11. 4 voices
12. 7 voices
13. 4 voices
14. 4 voices
15. 4 voices
16. 4 voices
17. 4 voices
18. 4 voices
19. 4 voices
20. 4 voices, with violins
21. 5 voices, with instruments
22. 4 voices
23. 4 voices
24. 4 voices
25. 4 voices
26. 4 voices
27. 4 voices
28. 4 voices
29. 4 voices
30. 4 voices
31.   solo, with instruments

32. 4 voices, without instruments
33. 4 voices
34. 8 voices, with violins
35. 8 voices, with violins

Regina Caeli without instruments

1. 4 voices
2. 4 voices
3. 8 voices
4. 4 voices
5. 6 voices
6. 4 voices
7. 4 voices
8. 4 voices
9. 4 voices
10. 4 voices
11. 4 voices, with organ continuo
12. 5 voices, with instruments

Litanies

1. 8 voices, with violins, for the votive processions

Motets without instruments

1. Duet, for the Sundays of the year
2. Duet, for the Apostles
3. Duet, for Pope and Confessor
4. 4 voices, for Peter of Alcantara
5. Duet, for the Sundays of the year
6. 6 voices, for the Sundays of the year
7. Solo, for the Virgin
8. Solo, for the Virgin and Martyr
9. 6 voices, for St. Joachim and St. Anne
10. 6 voices, for any feast of one or many saints
11. Solo, for St. John the Baptist
12. 4 voices, for the Blessed Trinity
13. 4 voices, for the Beheading of St. John the Baptist
14. Solo, for Confessor no Pope
15. Duet, for Sundays in Paschal Time
16. Solo, for Sundays after Epiphany
17. 6 voices, for Sunday in Paschal Time and during the year
18. Solo, for Confessor no Pope
19. 4 voices, for St. Mary Magdalen
20. Solo, for Confessor no Pope
21. 4 voices, for Palm Sunday
22. Duet, for a martyr
23. 4 voices, for St. Francis
24. 5 voices, for St. Thomas apostle

25. Solo, for James and Phillip apostles
26. 4 voices, for Santiago, patron of Spain
27. 4 voices, for the Dedication of the Church
28. Duet, for the Holy Name of Jesus
29. 4 voices, for St. Joseph
30. 4 voices, for the Transfiguration
31. 4 voices, for Resurrection and Sundays of the Paschal Time
32. 4 voices, votive
33. 6 voices, for the Betrothal and *Patrocinio* of the Blessed Virgin Mary
34. 4 voices, for Ildephonse
35. Duet, for the Sundays after Epiphany
36. 4 voices, for the Blessed Sacrament in the reformed Masses
37. 5 voices, for St. Mary Magdalen
38. 4 voices, for St. Andrew apostle
39. 4 voices, for St. Lucy
40. 7 voices, for St. Peter apostle
41. 4 voices, for St. Francis
42. Solo, for St. Joseph
43. 7 voices, for Sundays of the year
44. 4 voices, for the Blessed Virgin Mary
45. 4 voices, for the Blessed Virgin Mary
46. 4 voices, for the Blessed Virgin Mary
47. 4 voices, for the Blessed Virgin Mary
48. 4 voices, for the Blessed Virgin Mary
49. 5 voices, for the Assumption
50. 5 voices, for the Assumption
51. 6 voices, and soloist with organ continuo for the Blessed Virgin Mary
52. Solo, for the Blessed Virgin Mary
53. 8 voices, for the Blessed Virgin Mary
54. 8 voices, with organ continuo for the Blessed Virgin Mary
55. 4 voices, for the sorrows of the Blessed Virgin Mary
56. 4 voices, for the Visitation
57. 8 voices, for the Nativity and Conception (of Our Lord, Jesus Christ)
58. 2 choruses, for the Blessed Virgin Mary
59. 12 voices, for the Purification of the Blessed Virgin Mary
60. 8 voices, for the Purification of the Blessed Virgin Mary
61. 8 voices, for the Blessed Sacrament
62. 8 voices, for the Blessed Sacrament
63. 4 voices, for the Blessed Sacrament
64. 4 voices, for the Blessed Sacrament
65. Solo, for the Blessed Sacrament
66. Solo, for the Resurrection and Sunday of the Paschal Time
67. Duet, for the Innocent Saints and St. Justin, the Pastor
68. 4 voices, for the Holy Ghost
69. 8 voices, to Our Lord, Sundays of the year, and Holy Name of Jesus
70. 4 voices, for the apostles and martyrs of the Paschal Time

71. 4 voices, for the apostles and martyrs of the Paschal Time
72. Solo, for the apostles and martyrs of the Paschal Time
73. Solo, for Epiphany
74. 4 voices, for the Exaltation of the Cross
75. Solo, for the Exaltation of the Cross
76. 4 voices, for St. Gabriel
77. 6 voices, for the Ascension of Our Lord
78. 5 voices, for the sorrows of the Blessed Virgin Mary
79. 8 voices, for the Ascension of Our Lord

Motets with instruments

1. Solo, for the Purification of the Blessed Virgin Mary
2. Duet, for the Blessed Trinity
3. 4 voices, for St. Cyriacus and St. Paula
4. 5 voices, for the Holy Spirit
5. Solo, for the Blessed Sacrament
6. Duet, for the Blessed Sacrament
7. Duet, for the Blessed Sacrament
8. Duet, for the Blessed Sacrament
9. Solo, for the Resurrection and Sundays of the Paschal Time
10. Solo, for the Resurrection
11. Solo, for the Blessed Sacrament
12. Solo, for the Blessed Virgin Mary
13. Solo, for the Resurrection
14. 4 voices, for Confessor and Pope
15. Solo, for the Feast of All Saints
16. Solo, for the Ascension of Our Lord
17. Solo, for the Blessed Virgin Mary
18. Solo, for the Blessed Virgin Mary
19. Solo, for the Blessed Virgin Mary
20. Solo, for the Blessed Virgin Mary
21. Solo, for the Assumption of the Blessed Virgin Mary
22. 4 voices, for Maundy Thursday
23. 8 voices, for the Blessed Virgin Mary
24. 5 voices, for Christmas and Immaculate Conception
25. Duet, for Christmas and Immaculate Conception
26. Solo, for Christmas and Immaculate Conception
27. Solo, for Christmas and Immaculate Conception
28. Solo, for St. Peter apostle
29. Solo, for the Assumption of the Blessed Virgin Mary
30. 5 voices, for the Assumption of the Blessed Virgin Mary
31. Solo, for Santiago, Patron of Spain
32. Duet, for the Dedication of the Church
33. Solo, for the Dedication of the Church
34. Solo, for St. John the Baptist
35. Solo, for St. John the Baptist
36. Solo, for St. John the Baptist
37. Solo, for the Blessed Virgin Mary
38. Solo, for Christmas and Immaculate Conception

Works with Text in the Vernacular

Christmas Villancicos

1. 1733, originals missing
2. 1734, only 3 villancicos
3. 1735, missing 4 copies and the original of the villancico for the Epiphany
4. 1736, with originals and missing one copy
5. 1737, missing two originals
6. 1738, missing two originals
7. 1739, missing two originals
8. 1740, missing one original
9. 1741, all original and copies, complete[2]
10. 1742, complete
11. 1743, complete
12. 1744, complete
13. 1745, complete
14. 1746, missing one original and one copy
15. 1747, missing one original
16. 1748, missing one original and one copy
17. 1749, complete
18. 1750, missing two originals
19. 1751, complete
20. 1752, complete
21. 1753, missing one original
22. 1754, complete
23. 1755, complete
24. 1756, missing one original
25. 1757, complete
26. 1758, missing two originals
27. 1759, complete
28. 1760, complete (Note: Villancicos for the years 1761 and 1762 are missing)

Villancicos of the Immaculate Conception

1. 1733, without original
2. 1734, with originals
3. 1735, with originals
4. 1736, with originals
5. 1737, missing one original
6. 1738, with originals
7. 1739, with originals
8. 1740, with originals
9. 1741, with originals

---

2 Complete means that all originals and copies of the villancicos scores performed on a given occasion had been preserved.

10. 1742, with originals
11. 1743, with originals
12. 1744, with originals
13. 1745, with originals
14. 1746, with originals
15. 1747, missing one original
16. 1748, with originals
17. 1749, with originals
18. 1750, missing one original
19. 1751, complete
20. 1752, complete
21. 1753, complete
22. 1754, complete
23. 1755, complete
24. 1756, missing one original
25. 1757, complete
26. 1758, missing one copy
27. 1759, complete
28. 1760, complete (Note: The years 1761 and 1762 are missing.)

Works for the Blessed Sacrament

1. 14 calendas[3] with originals
2. 9 without originals
3. 30 villancicos for 4 voices, with originals
4. 11 without originals
5. 16 villancicos for 3, 6, 7, and 8 voices, with original
6. 46 arias, without originals
7. 15 with originals
8. 8 duets with originals
9. 19 without originals
10. 7 villancicos and 2 duets with originals
11. 8 villancicos and 4 solo arias, without originals

Unbound works with text in Latin

1. 7 voices, Magnificat
2. 8 voices, Magnificat
3. 8 voices, Dixit Dominus
4. 8 voices, Laudate Dominum
5. 8 voices, Credidi
6. 6 voices, Magnificat
7. 6 voices, Laudate Dominum
8. 6 voices, Laetatus sum
9. 7 voices, Laudate Dominum
10. 6 voices, Laetatus sum
11. 5 voices, Nunc dimitis
12. solo, Credidi

---

3 The *calenda* is the first or opening villancico of a set or series of villancicos.

13.   solo, Laudata Dominum
14.   6 voices, Beatus vir
15.   6 voices, Lauda Jerusalem
16.   6 voices, Lauda Jerusalem

Works bound in a choir book[4]

---

[4]   The choir book was not available for checking at the time of the research at the Malaga Cathedral. The beginning of the Inventory states that all works not so indicated by name, were written by Iribarren. Therefore, the writer assumes that the works bound in a choir book were written by Iribarren.

APPENDIX D

CATALOGUE OF ALL THE MANUSCRIPTS OF JUAN FRANCÉS DE IRIBARREN AVAILABLE IN THE MUSIC ARCHIVES OF THE MALAGA CATHEDRAL BASED ON THE FORMAT OF THE "THE 1770 MUSIC INVENTORY"

The manuscripts of Juan Francés de Iribarren available at the Music Library of the Malaga Cathedral are organized in bundles tied up with silk ribbons. The content of these bundles, called *legajos*, does not follow any systematic classification. A list provided by the Cathedral Library of the music contained in these *legajos* shows only the types of compositions included in each one of them without identifying the individual compositions.

From the beginning of this research, it became apparent that one of the goals of this study would have to be the cataloguing of Iribarren's works located at the Cathedral Library. The availability of the *1770 Inventario Musical*[1] discovered by Father A. Llordén offered, however, the possibility of pursuing this goal a step further. Therefore, by taking the 1770 musical inventory as a point of departure, it has been feasible to prepare a comparative catalogue between the compositions available at the Cathedral shortly after Iribarren's death and the works that are still preserved.

Different problems arose in the preparation of this catalogue. For the compositions with Latin texts, the 1770 musical inventory omits dates, seldom specifies instrumentations, and with the exception of the motets, does not indicate the performance occasion. For the compositions with vernacular texts, the 1770 inventory lists the dates only for the Immaculate Conception and Christmas villancicos; for the Blessed Sacrament works, only the types of compositions or the number of vocal parts, and instrumentation. The compositions available at the Cathedral were finally matched with almost all the items listed in the 1770 musical inventory.

Some minor changes were made in following the format of the 1770 musical inventory. Since the compositions for the Blessed Sacrament were not listed by years and there was not enough information to identify some of the items in subheadings 6 to 10 of the 1770 inventory, the compositions were regrouped into villancicos and arias. Thus, a more consistent cataloguing was reached for the compositions with vernacular texts.

As this study deals specifically with the villancicos of Juan Francés de Iribarren, it was found necessary to prepare, in addition to the comparative catalogue, an alphabetical catalogue of the incipits of all the villancicos available at the Malaga Cathedral.

In both catalogues, the titles of the compositions in the vernacular are spelled in current Spanish except for those in which a dialect is

---

[1] See Appendix C.

used. Duplicates of compositions with the same date are marked "D." For duplicates with a different date, the year is specified. The same text used in a different musical setting is also indicated. Compositions found in the Malaga Cathedral archives and not listed in the 1770 music inventory had been added to these catalogues and to the corresponding lists in the appendices. Compositions dated from the years 1763 to 1766 have also been listed although changes in style and music calligraphy in some of them creates doubt concerning the authenticity of the composer.

Masses with and without instruments

	Voices	*Instruments*	*Date*
1.	7	violins, trompas	1737
2.	7	violins	1734 D 1738
3.	8	violins	1738 D
4.	4	violins, bajon	1749 D
5.	4	violins, clarines	1749 D
6.	4	violins, trompas, bajon	1747 D
7.	4	violins, clarines, trompas, bajon	1745 D
8.	5	violins	1742
9.	4	violins (Duplicate scores for violin, oboe)	1738 D
10.	4	violin, oboes	1738
11.	2	violins	1763
12.	8	without instruments, based on the Cantate Domino	1737 D
13.	5	violins, trompas	1739
14.	4	organ continuo	1755
15.	5	without instruments, based on the hymn Caelestis Urbes	1734 D
16.	2 choruses		1756 D parts
17.	2 choruses	bajon	1761
18.	2 choruses and soloist		

Misereres with instruments

1.	6	violins	1749
2.	6	violins	1751
3.	6	oboe, flute recorder, trompas	1744
4.	6	violins	1750
5.	6	violins	1752
6.	6	violins, oboe, recorder, trompas, bajon	1745
7.	6	violins	1746
8.	6	violin, oboe, clarines, trompas, transverse flute, oboe de amor	1748
9.	6	violin, oboe, clarines, trompas, transverse flute	1749
10.	8	violins	1734

10.	8	violins	1734
11.	8	violins, oboes, recorder, trompas	1758 D
12.	4	recorders	1756
13.	8	violins	1738
14.	8	violins	1740
15.	8	violins	1736 D
16.	8	violins, transverse flute	1760
17.	8	violin, transverse flute, oboes, trompas	1756
18.	missing		

Misereres without instruments

19.	8		1758
	4		n.d.
20.	missing		
21.	missing		
22.	missing		

Lamentations for choruses and soloists for Wednesday of Holy Week

1.	7	violins, trompas	1752
2.	8	violins	1738
3.	7	violins, oboe, recorders, transverse flute (Duplicate scored for violins, oboes)	1743 D
4.	solo	violins, oboe	1735 D
5.	solo	violins	1740
6.	solo	violins, trompas	1747 D
7.	solo	violin, oboe, clarines, trompas	1751
8.	solo	violins	1738
9.	solo	violin, transverse flute, trompas	1747
10.	solo	violins, trompas	1753

Lamentations for choruses and soloists for Maundy Thursday

11.	7	violins, trompas, clarines	1752
12.	solo	transverse flute	1734
13.	solo	violins	1739
14.	solo	violins, trompas, clarines	1747
15.	solo	recorders	1750
16.	solo	violins, trompas	1754
17.	solo	violins	1735

Lamentations for soloists for Good Friday

18.	solo	violins	1746
19.	solo	—	1738
20.	solo	violins, trompas	1755
21.	solo	—	1739

Sequences with instruments[2]

1.	8	violins	1736 D
2.	8	violins	1735 D 1738
3.	5	violins	n.d.

Sequences without instruments

5.	solo	—	1756
8.	5	—	1734
11.	8	—	1738
12.	missing	—	
13.	solo, 2 choirs		1760
14.	5	—	1734 D
15.	solo	—	1745

Visperas with instruments for the Blessed Virgin Mary

1.	8	violins	1738
2.	6	violins	1737
3.	7	violins	1741
4.	6	violins, clarines, trompas	1754
5.	6	violins	1759

For Our Lord and Saints

6.	8	violins, clarines	1758
7.	6	violins, clarines, trompas	1748
8.	7	violins	1740
9.	8	violins	1738
10.	6	violins, clarines, trompas	1747

Complines

1.	8	—	1738
2.	5	violins	1743
3.	6	violins	1751
4.	6	violins	1761

---

[2] Numbers omitted are by other composers.

Te Deum laudamus with instruments

1.	8	violins	1737
2.	7	violins, clarines, trompas	1757

Vexilla Regis

1.	8	—	1739
2.	7	—	1751

Hymn for Corpus Christi

1.	4	Pange Lingua	1757

Office for the Dead, with and without instruments

1.	8	Office for the Dead	1738
2.	4	Office for the Dead	1744
3.	7	Mass	1758
4.	missing		
5.	missing		
6.	missing		
7.	missing		
8.	missing		
9.	missing		
10.	missing		
11.	8	Parce mihi	n.d.

Invitatories to the Nativity of Our Lord J.C.

1.	8	—	1737
2.	6	violins, trompa	1743
3.	8	violins, trompas	1746
4.	8	violins, trompas	n.d.
5.	7	violins, oboe	1733

Salves to the Blessed Virgin Mary with and without instruments

1.	5	violins, trompas	1755
2.	6	—	1738
3.	6	—	1761
4.	7	—	1740
5.	8	—	1738
6.	4	—	1749
7.	4	—	1765
8.	4	—	1744
9.	4	—	n.d.
10.	4	—	1738
11.	4	—	n.d.
12.	7	—	1741

13.	4	—	1745
14.	4	—	n.d.
15.	4	—	n.d.
16.	5	—	1733
17.	4	—	n.d.
18.	4	—	n.d.
19.	4	—	1763
20.	4	violins	1759
21.	5	violins, trompas	1738
22.	4	—	1753
23.	4	—	1738
24.	4	—	1743
25.	4	—	1739
26.	4	—	1757
27.	4	—	1754
28.	4	—	n.d.
29.	4	—	1752
30.	4	—	1738
31.	solo	violins, trompas	1752
32.	4	—	1748
33.	4	bajones, organo	1750
34.	8	violins	1734
35.	8	violins	1731

Regina Caeli, without instruments[3]

1.	4	—	1758
2.	4	bajon	1762
3.	8	—	1738
4.	4	—	1750
5.	6	—	n.d.
6.	4	—	1753
7.	4	—	1749
8.	4	—	1721
9.	4	—	1735
10.	4	—	1741
11.	4	organ continuo	1755
12.	5	violins, trompas	1748

Litany

1.	8	violins	1764

---

[3] Although these compositions were inventoried as without instruments, some of them are scored for instruments.

Motets without instruments

	Title	Date
1.	Omnia quae fecisti	1742
2.	Ibant apostoli	1748
3.	Ecce sacerdos magnus	1748
5.	Seraphim	1742
6.	Magna et mirabilia sunt	1737
7.	Simile est	1759
8.	Veni sponsa christi	1759
9.	O pax	1734 D
10.	Mirabilis Deus	1737
11.	Puer quinatus	1742
12.	Te invocamus	1732 D 1738
13.	Puer quinatus est nobis	1734 D 1739
14.	Domine iste sanctus	1746
15.	Christus Resurgens	1742
16.	Benedicam Dominum	1746
17.	Cantemus Domino	1753
18.	Iste est	1766
19.	For the Feast of Mary Magdalen	1734
20.	Domine quis havitavit	1765
21.	Vere languores	1747
22.	Gloria et honore	1746
23.	Franciscus Pauper	1739 2D
24.	Quia vidistime Thomas	1742
25.	Non turbetur	1755
26.	Iste est	1734 D 1738
27.	O quam metuendus	1734 D
28.	Domine Dominus noster	1740
29.	Memento igitur	1735
30.	Transfiguration of Our Lord, J.D.	1734 D 1738
31.	Surrexit Pastor	1734 D 1738
32.	Petite et accipietis	1753
33.	Cum esset desposata	1738
34.	O Ildephonse	1735
35.	For the Sundays after The Epiphany	1742
36.	O sacrum convivium	1758
37.	Pater superni Luminis	1738
38.	Beatus Andreas	1736 D 1738
39.	Columna es inmobilis	1736 D 1738
40.	Tu es Petrus	1741
41.	Franciscus	1733 2D 1751
42.	Te Joseph Celebrent	1745 2D
43.	Benedictus es Domine Deus	1758
44.	Tota pulchra es Maria	1740
45.	Sub tuum presidium	1741
46.	Ave Marie	1735
47.	Benedicta et venerabilis	1741
49.	Ad te clamo	1739

50.	Assumpta est Maria	1734 D 1738
51.	O Gloriosa Virginum	1757
52.	Beata es	1739
53.	For the feast of the most Holy Name of Mary	1737
54.	Plaudat nunc organis	1734 D 1738
56.	Exurgens Maris	1745
57.	Nativitas tua, Conceptio tua	1741
58.	For the feast of the most Holy Name of Mary	1761
59.	Hodie gloriosa	1728 D 1739
60.	Hodie gloriosa	1739
61.	O quam suavis	1741
62.	Ego sum panis vivus	1736 D 1738
63.	O quam suavis est Domine	1760
64.	O sacrum convivium	1755
65.	O salutaris hostia	1756
66.	Ecce vicit leo	1757
67.	Holy Innocents and St. Justin	1756
68.	Spiritus Domini	1738 D
69.	Benedictum est	1738
70.	Lux perpetua	1738
71.	Lux perpetua	1753
72.	Pretiosa	1742
73.	Reges Tharsis et insule	1760
74.	Dulce lignum	1734
75.	Dulce lignum	1755
76.	Misus est Angelus	1734 D 1738
77.	O Rex glorie	1757
78.	Doleo Superte	1738
79.	O Rex glorie	1741

Motets with instruments

	Title	Instrument	Date
1.	Hodie beata Virgo Maria	violin, trompa, bajón	1746
2.	Te invocamus	violins	1746
3.	Impij super iustos	violins, trompas, bajón	1745
4.	Cum complerentur	violins, clarines	1748
5.	O quam suavis	violins	1747
6.	Ego sum panis vivus	violins	1746
7.	Ego sum panis vivus	violins	1751
8.	O sacrum Convivium	violins, trompas	1747
9.	Ecce vicit leo	violins	1740
10.	Surrexit Pastor bonus	violin, clarines	1750
11.	O quam suavis est	violins, trompas	1751
12.	Virgo prudentissima	trompas, bajón	1744
13.	Ego dormivi	violins	1746
14.	Ecce sacerdos magnus	violins, clarines	1752
15.	O quam gloriosum	violins, trompas, bajón	1744
16.	O Rex glorie	violins, trompas, bajón	1745
17.	Tota pulchra	violins, trompas	1762

18.	Congratulamini mihi	violins, trompas	1753
19.	Sancta et immaculata	violins, trompas	1747
20.	Beata Dei genitrix Maria	violisn, trompas, bajón	1744
21.	Virgo prudentissima	violins	1753
22.	Sepulto Domino	transverse flute	1741 D
23.	Mater Dei	violins	1735 D 1738
24.	Conceptio tua, Nativitas tua	violins, clarines	1751
25.	Hodie concepta est, Hodie nata est	violins, trompas	1751
27.	Conceptio tua, Nativitas tua	violins	1749
28.	Tu es Petrus	violins, clarín, oboe	1744 2D
29.	Assumpta est Maria	violins, trompas	1747
30.	Virgo Prudentissima	violins	1739
31.	Iste est	trompas	1744
32.	O quam metuendus	violins	1763
33.	O quam metuendus est	violin, trompas	1749
34.	Puer quinatus est nobis	violins, clarines	1749
35.	Puer quinatus est nobis	violins	1754
36.	Puer quinatus est nobis	trompas	1744
37.	Beata es Virgo Maria	violins, trompas, bajón	1745
38.	Beatissime Virginis Maria	violins, trompas	1751

Christmas Villancicos

Date	Title	Voices	Instruments[4]	Type
1727	Predicó en Belén el cura	8	violins	
1733	Canten los jilguerilllos	2	transverse flute	
1733	Corred, corred los velos	7	violins, oboes	Calenda
1733	Mano a mano y sin pandero	7	—	
1733	Pues a navegar empieza Dios	5	bajoncillos	
1733	Pues está callando Bato	solo	—	
1733	Quien me dirá, como sabré	2	violins	Cantada
1733	Un rayo divino	6	violins, oboes	
1734	Jácara de fandanguillo	5	violins	Jácara
1734	La escala que vió Jacob	7	violins	
1734	Resuenen estruendos	8	violins	Calenda
1734	Si a nosotros se ha dado el hijo	4	violins	
1734	Una señora de manto	7	violins, oboes	
1734	Vaya de placer	8	violins	
1735	Al portal con gran donaire	8	violins	Cantada
1735	Niño agraciado	solo	violins	
1735	Los pastores de Belén	8	violins	
1735	Resonando a Isaías	8	violins	Calenda
1736	A Belén caminad	2	violins	Calenda
1736	De Belén los carpinteros	6	violins	Cantada

[4] All the villancicos have continuo; therefore, only the non-continuo instruments are listed.

111

Year	Title	Number	Instruments	Type
1736	El herrador de Belén	5	—	Tonadilla
1736	Ha de haber tonada	8	violins	
1736	Tres campeones de oriente	8	violins	
1736	Viendo que las novedades	6	—	
1736	Oyendo un pajarote	solo	violins, oboes	Cantada
1736	Oyes Hipolito	2	violins	Calenda
1736	Prisioneros alentad	8	violins	
1737	Al baile mañonas	8	violins	Tonadilla
1737	Al ver al Niño monarca	5	violins, oboes	
1737	Como Pasqual en la corte	5	bajones	
1737	Con mirra, incienso y oro	8	violins, oboes	
1737	En el Aranjuez del mundo	8	violins	
1737	Esta noche al portal vienen	4	violins	
1737	Desde Málaga esta noche	8	violins, oboes	
1737	Dígame, dígame	2	violins	Cantada
1737	Fogosa inteligencia	2	violins	Cantada
1737	Tortolilla que amorosa	2	violins, oboe	Cantada
1737	Un crítico y un pastor	6	violins, oboe	
1737	Venga incendio soberano	8	violins	Calenda
1738	Adonde gallego	2	violins, oboe	
1738	A los maestros que sabios	8	violins	
1738	De Belén los oficiales	8	violins	
1738	Oh bienaventurada	solo	violins	Cantada
1738	Montados en sus esdrújulos	2	bajón or violin	
1738	Por las calles buscando	5	violins	

Year	Title		Instruments	Genre
1738	Sabiendo que en nochebuena	8	violins	Tonadilla
1738	Triste lamenta Israel	8	violins	Calenda
1738	Viniendo a Belén los reyes	6	violins	De Negros
1739	Apaltense digo	5	violins	
1739	Camina Antón	2	violins	
1739	Cesen desde hoy los profetas	8	violins	Calenda
1739	Los marineros de flota	8	violins	Tonadilla
1739	Serranillas a bailar	6	bajoncillos	
1739	Siendo influjo el ardor de una llama	4	violins	De Reyes
1739	Silvio soy, músico antiguo	solo	violins	Cantada
1739	Un pastorcillo italiano	6	violins, oboe	
1739	Un sobrio y un comilón	2	bajones	
1740	Corriendo zagales	5	violins, oboes	Vizcaino
1740	Dos astrólogos	2	violins	
1740	Ha de Nembroth el bárbaro edificio	8	violins, oboe, clarin	Calenda
1740	Por no faltar a la moda	8	violins, oboe	Tonadilla
1740	Toribión un Asturiano	5	bajones	Asturiano
1740	Vamo culendita	3	violins, oboes	De Negros
1740	Vamos, vamos partorcillos	4	transverse flutes	
1740	Yo y dos brutos esta noche	solo	bajones	Cantada
1740	Zagales venid	7	violins, oboes	De Reyes
1741	Alma mía	5	bajones, transverse flute	
1741	Aquella común borrasca	8	violins, oboe	Calenda
1741	Bostezando vas Antón	5	bajones	
1741	Como son las tonadillas	9	bajoncillos	Tonadilla

Year	Title	Voices	Instruments	Genre
1741	Esta noche con gracejo	7	violins, oboes	Tonadilla
1741	Hasta aquí Dios amante	solo	violins, oboes	Cantada
1741	Hola pastorcillos	7	violins, oboes	Pastorela
1741	Que habreis primero vos	2	violins	Cantada
1741	Ay que presurosos	4	violins, oboe	De Reyes
1742	Andemos aprisa	2	violins	
1742	Cantando y bailando	6	bajoncillo	
1742	Como hoy en público vienen	4	violins	De Reyes
1742	En tanto que los zagales	4	bajones	
1742	Nevado albergue de un amor bizarro	solo	violins	Cantada
1742	Por una deuda en prisiones	8	violins	Calenda
1742	Un festín soberano	7	violins	Canción
1742	Unas lavanderas vienen	3	violins	
1742	Vaya de tonadilla	5	transverse flutes	Tonadilla
1743	A alegrar a mi Niño	solo	violins	
1743	Buscando al recién nacido	6	violins	Tonadilla
1743	El retrato del Niño	solo	violins	
1743	En Belén los bordadores	7	violins	Tonadilla
1743	Has visto Gila de esa luz la llama	2	violins	De Reyes
1743	Helmana Flancisca	6	bajoncillos	De Negros
1743	Montes tenedme envidia	solo	violins	Cantada
1743	Ven nuevo Gedeón	7	violins, oboe, transverse flute	Calenda
1743	Viendo el Niño	7	violins	Tonadilla
1744	A la hoguera pastorcillos	7	violins, trompas, bajón	Tonadilla
1744	El comilón honrado	solo	violins	Cantada

114

1744	Los zagales a Fileno	5	violins	Tonadilla
1744	Mirando humano al Niño	8	violins, trompas, bajón	Pastorela
1744	Oyenos la fina canción	2	bajoncillos	
1744	Para celebrar la noche	5	violins	Tonadilla
1744	Qué alegre caminas	2	violins	De Reyes
1744	Qué tempestad los orbes	7	violins, oboe, clarines, bajón, trompas, transverse flute	
1744	Zagales, como una Pascua me vengo	5	violins	Calenda
1745	Al portal las montañesas	8	violins	Jácara
1745	Andar, andar y el gozo se explaye	5	violins, trompas, bajón	Tonadilla
1745	Del universal presidio	7	violins, trompas, clarines	Calenda
1745	Festivas zagalas	5	violins	Tonadilla
1745	Oiga Señor mío	2	bajoncillos, recorder	
1745	Para reclutar soldados	5	violín, trompas, bajón	
1745	Que asombro zagales	6	violín, oboe, clarines, trompas, transverse flute	De Reyes
1745	Siendo pastor de fama	solo	violins, clarín	Cantada
1745	Viendo que Jil hizo raya	6	violins, violón	Jácara
1745	A Belén Bartola	2	violins	
1746	Aquel primitivo incendio	6	violins, transverse flute, oboes, trompas, clarines	Calenda
1746	Camaradas a bailar	6	violins, trompas	
1746	Camaradas, pues la noche			
1746	Las zagales de la corte	6	violins, bajón	Tonadilla
1746	Que es lo que traes Silvia	5	violins	Tonadilla
1746	Que temprano bien mío	solo	violins	Cantada
1746	Señora parida yo soy un pastor	solo	violins	Cantada

115

1746	Serranillas esta noche	5	violins, trompas, bajón	Tonadilla
1747	Cierta tropa de chiquillas	4	violins, oboes de amor	Jácara
1747	Ha de haber jácara buena	6	violins	Cantada
1747	Hola chiquillo	solo	violins	Calenda
1747	La humana Babilonia	6	violins, transverse flutes, clarines, trompas	Tonadilla
1747	La tonadilla graviosa	6	violins, trompas	
1747	Noticia Bartolo	5	violins, trompas	
1747	Oi tres baterías	7	violins, clarines, oboe, trompas, transverse flute	De Reyes
1747	Pastorelilla aquí	2	violins	Pastorela
1747	Peregrinas al portal	7	violins, trompas	Tonadilla
1748	A la divina pastora	4	violins	Pastorela
1748	Cantad al son del clarín	6	violins, oboe, clarines, trompas	Calenda
1748	Coriendo zagalas	6	violins, trompas	Tonadilla
1748	Echo al aire un mar de luces	4	violins, clarines, trompas	De Reyes
1748	Hala, hala, que el cielo	4	oboes, clarines, trompas, bajones	De Reyes
1748	Muchachas al baile	3	violins, transverse flute	Tonadilla
1748	Nuevo Balsaín le ofrece	6	violins	Tonadilla
1748	Vamos claros mi Niño yo bailando	solo	violins	Cantada
1748	Vaya de jácara	5	violin, recorders	Jácara
1749	A Belén pastorcillos	7	violins, trompas	Tonadilla
1749	Al portal panderillas	3	violins	Tonadilla
1749	Así chocorrotiya	solo	violins, bajoncillos, bajón, transverse flute	De Negros
1749	Como en Belén está el sabio	2	violins	
1749	Enojado con el mundo	3	violins	
1749	Hacer quiere una comedia Jil	4	violins	

116

1749	Nueva armonía	8	violin, oboe, clarines, trompas	Calenda
1749	Pastores a un lado	4	violins	De Reyes
1749	Reparad zagales	7	violin, oboe, clarines, trompas, transverse flute	Tonadilla
1749	Seguidillas muchachos	7	violins	Tonadilla
1750	Al son de sus caracolas	7	violins, trompas	
1750	Bello atractivo	solo	recorders	
1750	Digo que no he de cantarla	5	violins	Jácara
1750	Las gitanas bulliciosas	7	violins	Tonadilla
1750	Para divertir al Niño	7	violins, trompas de caza	Tonadilla
1750	Que es esto cielos	solo	violins	Cantada
1750	Querubes del trono	6	violins, clarines, trompas	Calenda
1750	Viendo un seise a dos zagales	3	violins	
1751	Con tenebras	6	violins	
1751	Eschuchad moradores del orbe	7	violin, oboe, clarines	Calenda
1751	Hola Jau	2	violins, transverse flute	Cantada
1751	La pastora Jileta	7	violins	Tonadilla
1751	Pastorelica de bella invención	7	violins, trompas	De Reyes
1751	*Pax di orbe*	solo	violins, oboe	Cantada
1751	Toribio, noble asturiano	6	violins	Tonadilla
1751	Un pajarero contento	6	violins	Tonadilla
1751	Vaya de jácara	6	violins	Jácara
1752	Atención que de un navío	4	violins, oboe	De Negros
1752	Angélicas milicias	8	violins, oboes, trompas, clarines	Calenda
1752	Dos pastorcillos soldados	2	violins, oboes, trompas, piccolo	
1752	Ea! Anfriso alegre	7	violins	Tonadilla

1752	La noche se ostenta	4	violins, clarines, trompas	De Reyes
1752	Las tiernas pastorcillas	7	violins, trompas	Pastorela
1752	Las zagalas de Belén	8	violins, trompas	Tonadilla
1752	Para hacer burla del Diablo	3	violins	Tonadilla
1752	Toquen los clarines	8	violins, clarines	Jácara
1752	Con júbilo tierno	7	violins, trompas, clarines	De Reyes
1753	A la palabra nacida	3	violins	
1753	Esta noche lo Neglillo	6	violins, oboe, trompas	De Negros
1753	De Belén las pastoras	5	violins, trompas	Tonadilla
1753	En el portal van entrado	5	violins	Tonadilla
1753	Pastores de Belén	5	violins, trompas	Tonadilla
1753	Per Maria Gratia plena	solo	violins	Cantada
1753	Respira Adán	solo	violins	Cantada
1753	Zagales corred	8	violin, oboe, trompas, clarines	Calenda
1754	A una estrella luminosa	7	violin, clarines	De Reyes
1754	Batillo con su mujer	2	violins, trompas	Pastorela
1754	La zagaleja Mirtila	4	violin, transverse flute	
1754	Los orbes celestiales	solo	violins, trompas	Cantada
1754	Montes de Palestina	7	violins, clarines, trompas	Calenda
1754	Un danzante mi niño	solo	violins, transverse flute, oboe	Juguete
1754	Un gallardo portugués	5	violins	Portugués
1754	Un siciliano festivo	7	violins, trompas	Siciliano
1754	Vengan los pastorcillos	5	violins	Tonadilla
1755	Andar estrellitas	7	violins, trompas	De Reyes
1755	Bato y Pasquala contentos	8	violins, piccolo	Tonadilla

118

Year	Title		Instrumentation	Genre
1755	En tierra y en abismo	8	violins, trompas, clarines	Calenda
1755	Guapo ha de ser el tonillo	5	violins	Jácara
1755	Jerusalén eleva	solo	violins, trompas	Cantada
1755	Los chiquillos de Belén	4	violins	
1755	Los gallegos enfadados	6	violins, oboe, chirimía	
1755	Los plateros de Belén	8	violins, trompas	
1755	Oigan que una peregrina	4	violins	Tonadilla
1755	Un zagalillo	4	violins, oboe, transverse flute	
1755	Zás, jacarilla en campaña			Jácara
1756	Antonillo un negro alegre	3	violins, flautino, oboe	De Negro
1756	Dos zagalas de Belén	2	violins	
1756	Fuera, fuera que a Belén	2	violins, transverse flute, piccolo	
1756	Hala, hala que el cielo	8	violins, clarines	De Reyes
1756	Oh que bien que suspenden	solo	violins, trompas	Cantada
1756	Oigan una tonadilla	5	violins	Tonadilla
1756	Piedad inmenso Dios	8	violins, recorder, oboe, trompa	Calenda
1756	Vamos aprisa pastores	6	violins, oboes, trompas	Pastorela
1756	Vaya de tonadilla	8	violins, clarines, trompas	Tonadilla
1757	Alarma, alarma	8	violins, clarines	De Reyes
1757	De Belén los pastorcillos	3	violins, piccolo, trompas, clarines	
1757	Hola pastores, que sonoro acento	solo	violins, trompas	Cantada
1757	Jacarilla en campaña	5	violins	Jácara
1757	La naturaleza humana	8	violins, trompas	Calenda
1757	Una pastorcilla amante	5	violins, trompas	Tonadilla
1757	Ya, oh gran naturaleza	2	violins, recorder, oboes	Cantada

119

Year	Title		Instrumentation	Genre
1757	Ya que el Niño hermoso	5	violins, trompas	Pastorela
1758	Abandonados cautivos	8	violins, transverse flute, oboe, trompas, clarines	Calenda
1758	Con rutilante armonía	7	violins, trompas	De Reyes
1758	Esta noche al Niño hermoso	7	violins	Tonadilla
1758	Hombres prevenid puro	2	violins, trompas	Cantada
1758	Oh! que halagueña canción	2	violins, trompas	Cantada
1758	Pensativa una pastora	5	violins	Tonadilla
1758	Puesto que antaño dió gusto	7	violins, booe, chirimía	
1758	Que es esto amor que ves!	solo	violins, oboe, transverse flute, trompas	Cantada
1758	Ya anticipo la alegre primavera	solo	violins	
1759	Ay tierno pastor mío	solo	violins, oboe, trompas	Cantada
1759	Companela queridiya	3	violins, oboe	De Negro
1759	Esta noche es noche buena	7	violins, transverse flute	Tonadilla
1759	Oí tres Reyes juntos	7	violins, oboe, clarines	De Reyes
1759	Pastores volad	7	violins, clarines	De Reyes
1759	Por aquel horizonte	2	violins, oboe, trompas	Cantada
1759	Todo confusión el mundo	8	violins, oboes, chirimía	Calenda
1759	Toribio con sus zagales	7	violins, flautinos	
1759	Vaya, vaya jacarilla	solo	violins	Jácara
1759	Venga tonadilla venga	7	violins	Tonadilla
1760	Cerrando la Mogiganga	8	violin, chirimía, clarines	
1760	Corriendo una pastorcilla	6	violins, recorders	Tonadilla
1760	Cuando Señor, será el día	7	violins, trompas, clarines	Calenda
1760	Del fenix del cielo	5	violins, oboe	De Reyes
1760	El concejo de Belén	7	violins, trompas	

Date	Title	Voices	Instruments	Type
1760	Fuera, fuera que a Belén	4	violins, chirimía	Cantada
1760	Mil veces sea bendito	solo	violins, clarines, trompas	Jácara
1760	Porque en la entrada festiva	4	violins	
1760	Un pastor muy jacarero	7	violins, recorder	

Immaculate Conception Villancicos

Date	Title	Voices	Instruments	Type
1733	En las aras en quien admiramos	solo	violins	Cantada
1733	Pues eterno el día	4	violins, oboe	
1733	Que armoniosa consonancia	8	violins	
1733	Venid al aplauso	7	violins	
1734	Con júbilo amante	4	bajones, transverse flutes	
1734	La gloria de admire	8	violins	Calenda
1735	A retirar sus tropas	8	violins	Calenda
1735	Diluvios de gracias	4	violins	
1736	Quien será un prodigio	8	violins	Calenda
1736	Siendo las obras	4	violins	
1736	Acudid mortales	4	violins	
1737	Aun asombro convoca la gracia	8	violins	Calenda
1737	Graciosa y célebre	4	violins	
1737	Que milagro, que portento	2	violins	Cantada
1738	Recoged las velas	8	violins	Calenda
1738	Clarines del día	2	violins	
1739	Calme el viento	8	violins	Calenda

1739	Cediendo a la gracia	4	violins	
1739	La Fiera en el monte	3	violins	
1740	Pues ya la serpiente	4	violins, oboes	Calenda
1740	Dirás plausibles	7	violins, oboes	Cantada
1740	Delicioso clavel	2	violins, transverse flutes	Calenda
1741	Saluden al alba	7	violins, oboes	Cantada
1741	La mas graciosa nave	2	violins, oboe	
1741	Fuego, fuego	4	violins, oboe	
1742	Alégrese la tierra	2	violins	Cantada
1742	Gire la bélica voz	7	violins	Calenda
1742	Quien me dirá con primor	3	violins	
1743	Deseando cantar juntos	solo	violins	
1743	Las dulces Filomenas	7	violins, oboes, trompa, bajón	Calenda
1743	Silva culebra infernal	2	violins	Cantada
1744	Háganle salve liras armoniosas	6	violins, clarines, trompas	Calenda
1744	A coger delicias	2	violins, oboe, transverse flute	Cantada
1744	Guerra pública el día	4	violins,oboe, clarín, trompa, bajón	Cantada
1745	Que embarcación la playa	6	violin, oboe, trompas, clarines, bajón	Calenda
1745	Electa para el bién	solo	violins, oboes, trompas, bajón, transverse flutes	Cantada
1745	Oiga Bella Niña	5	violins, trompas, bajón	Calenda
1746	Huya infiel serpiente	3	violins, clarines, trompas	
1746	A la Niña hermosa	5	transverse flutes	
1748	Acordes sirenas	6	violins, clarines, trompas	Calenda
1748	Al repique de la aurora	solo	violins, clarines	Cantada
1748	Pajarito soy con alma	solo	recorders	Cantada

1749	En purezas y gracias	4	violin, oboe, trompas, recorder, clarines	Calenda
1749	De laja el prodigiosa	7	violins, trompas	Cantada
1749	Línea señaló Dios	solo	violin, oboe, clarines	
1750	Huyan las sombras	5	violins, trompas, clarines	Calenda
1750	La ciudad que en Pathmos vió	7	violins, trompas	Cantada
1750	Respira sin temor naturaleza	solo	violins, transverse flute	Cantada
1755	Ay, que triunfante	solo	violins, trompas, clarines	Calenda
1755	Hoy en un cielo nuevo	7	violins, oboe, trompas, flautino	
1755	Que asombro que maravilla!	4	violins, oboes, trompas, transverse flute	
1757	A la vara florida	3	violins	
1757	Sagrada devoción	solo	violins, recorders	Cantada
1758	Alégrese toda la naturaleza	8	violins, clarines	Calenda
1758	Del primer hombre por esa culpa fiera	solo		Cantada
1758	A la Niña del pueblo escogido	4	violins	Cantada
1759	Es inmutable Dios omnipotente	solo	violins, clarines	
1759	Gracia y naturaleza	7	violins, chirimía, oboe	Calenda
1759	Ha de la informe mansión	7	violins, oboe, trompas	Calenda
1760	Oigan los campos de Booz	6	violins, trompas	
1760	Hermosa Ruth, por serlo	3,8	violins, oboe	
1760	Pues que Ruth a los campos	9	violins	
1763	Clarines de las selvas			Calenda
1763	Es María tan pura	6	violins	
1763	Montes y riscos			Cantada
1764	Jardinera serpiente	2	violins	
1765	Arda, pues, la fineza			

123

1765   Pulcra Ester privilegiada

1765 — Sol es María, que con luz ardiente

Villancicos for the Blessed Sacrament

Date	Title	Voices	Instruments	Type
1720	Cuando vayando vuelven	2	violins	
1720	Quien nos dirá de una flor	4	violins	
1720	Buscando la gala	2	violins	
1720	Prosigue acorde lira	solo	violins	Cantada
1729	Violines rompió a nombre	8	violins, oboes	
1734	A los bullicios del aura	4	violins	
1734	Al arma	4	violins	
1734	Ay sagrado cupido	4	violins	
1734	Conozca mi ventura	solo	violins, oboes	Cantada
1735	Como el amor infinito	8	violins	Calenda
1735	Dando al aire más aliento	4	violins	
1735	En el día del Señor	6		
1735	Tremolen sus banderas	4	violins	
1736	Canoras aves	4	violins	
1736	Con que dulzura el alma	2	violins	Cantada
1736	Si para darme ese Pan	2	violins	Cantada
1737	A la gala de aquel disfraz	8		
1737	Al altar divino	8	violins, oboes	Calenda
1737	Al célebre combate	8	violins, oboes, clarines	

124

1737	Al dulce alimento	8	violins	Cantada
1737	Al himno soberano	2	violins	Calenda
1737	Armonioso regio estruendo	8	violins	Cantada
1737	Aunque se oculta en sendales	solo	violins, oboes	
1737	Ay que alegre, festivo	4	violins	
1737	Camina corazón	solo	violins, clarines	Cantada
1737	Corazón venturoso	7	violins	
1737	De amor la oficina	4	violins, oboes	
1737	De la nube fecunda	4	violins	
1737	Dulces teorbas	4	violins	
1737	En agua y con tierra	4	violins	
1737	En círculo abreviado	solo	violins	Cantada
1737	En las ardientes alas	4	violins	
1737	Los pájaros, los troncos	solo	violins	Cantada
1737	Marinero que zurcas	4	violins	
1737	Por más que soberbio	4	violins	
1737	Pues en ese panal	solo	viola	Cantada
1737	Resuenen los ecos	4	violins	
1737	Vamos coriendo a buscar	4	violins	
1737	Vaya de parabienes	4	violins	
1738	A una empresa divina	4	violins	
1738	Al golfo del mundo	4	violins	
1738	De amor exceso amante	solo	violins, oboes, viola	Cantada
1738	Haciendo fiel seña	8	violins	Calenda
1738	Llévame los ojos	4	violins	

1738	Preste vuelos amor	solo	violins	Cantada
1738	Que bien abejuelas	4	violins	De Reyes
1738	Volver al Niño monarca	8	violins	Calenda
1739	A competir a esas aras	8	violins	
1739	Al eco asombroso	4	violins	
1739	Ay que alegre	2	violins	Cantada
1739	Es el poder del hombre	2	violins	Cantada
1739	La Armonía de las aves	4	violins	
1739	Marinerillo		violins, oboes	
1739	Operarios a segar	4	violins	
1739	Para aplaudir al señor	8	violins	Tonadilla
1740	Vuele, a ese incendio	2	violins	Cantada
1740	Huyendo la ruina	8	violins	Calenda
1741	Como podrá mi lengua	2	violins, oboes, transverse flute	Cantada
1741	En el claro cristal	4	violins, oboe	
1741	Labrador oficioso deja	4	violins	
1741	Llegando a la Troxes	7	violins, oboe	Calenda
1741	Siguiendo los giros	4	violins, oboe	
1742	A labrar	4	violins	
1742	Amor primoroso	4	violins	
1742	Ay jardinero	2	violins	
1742	Haga a Leva la señal	8	violins, oboes	Calenda
1742	Que misterio	solo	violins	Cantada
1743	A coger los flores	solo	violins, oboe	Cantada
1743	Ay maravilla de los corazones	7	violins, oboe	Calenda

Year	Title	Voices	Instruments	Type
1743	Que alegría	4	violins	
1744	Cual nave de las olas combatida	solo	violins, recorder, transverse flute, oboe	Cantada
1744	Dando a la playa	2	violins	
1744	Hoy canción traemos	6	violins	Tonadilla
1744	La salva le hagamos	4	violins, trompas	
1744	Llenando de alegrías	4	violins	
1744	Oí a ese corderito		violins	Tonada
1745	A pelear nobles deseos	6	violins, oboe, clarines	
1745	Feliz el alma ansiosa	solo	violins, trompas, bajón	Cantada
1745	Que azucena	4	violins, clarines, trompas, bajón	
1746	Corred almas felices	6	violin, clarines, trompas, bajón	
1746	Cual suele placentero	2	violin, clarines	Cantada
1746	Deja que esas flechas	4	violins	
1746	Rayando el alba	4	violins	
1746	Sabia extensión	solo	violins	
1747	A gozar mortales	4	violins	
1747	De nuevo la aurora	2	violin, trompas	
1747	En esas aras	solo	violins	Cantada
1747	Fábrica soberana	6	violins, trompas	
1747	Gozosa el alma	4	violin, clarines	
1747	Ya llegando Señor	solo	violins, trompas	Cantada
1748	Acelera los pasos	4	violins, clarines	
1748	La dulzura mayor	solo	violins, clarines	Cantada
1748	Vesubio soberano	solo	violins, trompas	Cantada
1748	Canoras aves	solo	violins, trompas	Cantada

1748	Suspende ya los vuelos	2	violins	
1748	Esa cumbre excelente	6	violins, clarines	
1749	Labrador divino	4	violin, oboe, clarines	
1749	Logra el valle	2	violins	Cantada
1749	Oí Señor soberano	solo	recorders	Cantada
1749	Quien no admira	solo	violin, trompas	Cantada
1749	Serafines que en el trono	6	violins, trompas	
1750	Al pan misterioso	4	violins, clarines	
1750	Al manantial precioso	4	violins, trompas	
1750	Como el ciervo	solo	violins	Cantada
1750	Haga salva canora	7	violins, trompas, clarines	Calenda
1750	Muestra zéfiro amante	3	violin, clarines	
1750	Que le diremos	2	violins	
1750	Si alabarte solicito	2	violins	Cantada
1751	Milagro admiración	7	violins, trompas	
1751	Porque dichas del cielo	4	violins, clarines	
1751	Salve oh Señor augusto	solo	violins, clarines	Cantada
1751	Al festejo singular	4	violins, trompas	
1751	Aquel Divino Amante	2	violin, transverse flute	Cantada
1752	Canoras serafines	4	violins, clarines	
1752	Celebremos festivos	2	violins, oboe	Juguete
1752	En esa dulce hoguera	7	violin, oboe, clarines, trompas	Calenda
1753	Al son de festivas trompas	7	violins, trompas, clarines	Calenda
1753	Corred almas puras	4	violins, clarines	
1753	Oh pan sacramentado	7	violins, clarines	

128

Año	Título		Instrumentación	Tipo
1754	Alados celestiales	7	violins, oboe, trompas, clarines	Calenda
1754	Inmenso Dios	solo	violins, trompas	Cantada
1754	Las hojas se mueven	4	violins, trompas, clarines	Cantada
1754	Oh fogoso volcan	solo	violins, trompas	Calenda
1755	Al agua tritones	8	violins, clarines	Cantada
1756	A la mesa del cielo	solo	violins, oboe, recorder, trompas	Cantada
1756	Aplaudan	2	violin, transverse flute	Cantada
1756	En esta sacra mesa	2	violins, clarines	Cantada
1756	Esta es aquella mesa	2	violins, piccolo, trompas	Cantada
1756	Las aves acordes	8	violins, oboe, recorder, trompas	Calenda
1756	Toda de luces	solo	violin, recorder, trompas	Cantada
1757	Alentad oh mortales	2	violins, oboe, trompas	Cantada
1757	Exceso es del amor	solo	violins	Cantada
1757	Hoy entre la blancura	solo	violins, oboe, transverse flute	Cantada
1757	Renazcan los campos	2	violins, oboes, trompas, recorder	Cantada
1757	Vengan hoy al combate	7	violin, oboes, trompas, recorder	Calenda
1757	Yo soy aquel furor	2	violins, oboe, transverse flute, clarines, trompas	Cantada
1758	Bendecid al Señor	2	violins, trompas	Cantada
1758	Dulce prenda del cielo	8	violins, oboe, trompas	Calenda
1758	La abejuela misteriosa	4	violins	
1758	Llega paloma	2	violins, oboe, trompas	Cantada
1758	Todo viene de vos	solo	violins, trompas	Cantada
1759	En el centro feliz	solo	transverse flute	Cantada
1759	Un grano misterioso	7	violins, trompas	Calenda
1760	Todo mortal constante	6	violins, trompas	Calenda

Arias and Duets for the Blessed Sacrament

Date	Title	Voices	Instruments
1734	Gitanillas gitanas	2	violins
1738	Sagrado caudillo	2	violins
1740	Vuele a ese incendio	2	violins
1744	Yo quisiera ser clarín	2	violins
1745	Hortelanito hermoso	solo	violins
1748	Piadosamente divino	solo	recorders
1749	Los ámbitos pueble	2	violins, clarines
1750	Ya se que en Pan te ocultas	solo	recorders
1751	Arde el furor intrépido	solo	violins, trompas
1751	Manjar divino	solo	violins, trompas
1751	Que fina y ansiosa	solo	violins, viola
1752	Clisie amante	2	violins, trompas
1752	Hostia amante	2	violins, trompas
1752	La cierva herida	solo	violins
1752	Perlas desata fluida	solo	violins, clarines
1753	Admite dueño amado	solo	violins
1753	Ave de bronce marcial	solo	violins, clarines
1753	Ya cesa la tormenta	solo	violins, oboes, trompas
1754	A ti mi Dios adora	solo	violins, flute
1754	Sus gozos explicando	solo	violins, trompas
1755	A quien mi Dios amado	solo	violins, trompas

130

1755	Dios amable	solo	violins
1755	Si el mar por celoso	solo	violins, trompas
1755	Sois mi Dios	solo	violins
1755	Vesubio soberano	solo	violins
1759	Todo es gozo	solo	violins
1760	Bello esposo, dulce amante	solo	recorders
1760	Todo el mundo en alborozo	solo	flutes

APPENDIX E

ALPHABETICAL CATALOGUE OF THE VILLANCICOS BY JUAN FRANCÉS de IRIBARREN AVAILABLE AT THE MALAGA CATHEDRAL IN 1973[1]

A alegrar a mi niño	1743
A Belén Bartola	1746 D
A Belén caminad	1736
A Belén pastorcillas	1749 D
A coger delicias	1744 D 1768
A coger las flores	1743
A competir a esas aras	1739
A de haber tonada	1736
A donde gallego	1738
A gozar mortales	1747
A la divina pastora	1748 D
A la gala de aquel disfraz	1737
A la hoguera pastorcillos	1744 D
A la mesa del cielo	1756
A la Niña del pueblo escogido	1758 D
A la Niña hermosa	1744 1746
A la palabra nacida	1753
A la vara florida	1757
A labrar	1742
A los bullicios del aura	1734
A los maestros que sabios	1738 D
A pelear nobles deseos	1745
A quien mi Dios amado	1755
A retirar sus tropas	1735
A una empresa divina	1738
A una estrella luminosa	1754
Abandonados cautivos	1758 D
Acelera los pasos	1748
Acordes sirenas	1748
Acudid mortales	1736 D
Al agua tritones	1755
Al altar divino	1737
Al arma	1734
Al baile miñonas	1737 D
Al célebre combate	1737 2D 1738
Al chocorrotiya puz	1749 D
Al dulce alimento	1737 D 1738
Al eco asombroso	1739
Al festejo singular	1751

---

[1] All titles are spelled in current Spanish except for those which are written in dialects or foreign language. Two compositions listed under the same title indicates a different musical setting. Duplicates of compositions with the same date are marked "D." For duplicates with a different date, the year is specified.

Buscando al recién nacido	1743 D
Buscando la gala	1720 D
Calme el viento	1739
Camaradas a bailar	1746 2D
	1748 D 1766
Camaradas pues la noche	1746
Camina Antón	1739 D
Camina corazón	1737
Canoras aves	1736 D 1737
Canoras aves	1748
Canoras serafines	1752
Cantad al son del clarín	1748 2D 1766
Cantando y bailando	1742 D
Canten los jilguerillos	1733
Cediendo a la gracia	1739
Celebremos festivos	1752
Cesen desde hoy los profetas	1739 D
Cerrando la mogiganga	1760 3D
Cierta tropa de chiquillas	1747
Clarines de las selvas	1763
Clarines del día	1738 D
Como Dios del otro mundo	1766
Como el amor infinito	1735 D 1738
Como el ciervo	1750
Como en Belén está el sabio	1749 D
Como hoy en público vienen	1743 D 1742
Como Pascual en la corte	1737 2D
Como podrá mi lengua	1741
Como son las tonadillas	1741 D
Companela queridiya	1759 D
Con júbilo amante	1734
Con júbilo tierno	1752 D
Con mi ganado estaba	1766
Con mirra, incienso y oro	1737 D
Con que dulzura el alma	1736
Con rutilante armonía	1758 D 1755 1764
Con tenebras	1751
Conozca mi ventura	1734
Corazón venturoso	1737 D
Corred almas felices	1746
Corred almas puras	1753
Corred, corred los velos	1733 2D
Corriendo una pastorcilla	1760 D
Corriendo zagalas	1748 2D 1766
Corriendo zagales	1740 D
Cual nave de las olas combatida	1744
Cual suele placentero	1746
Cuando Señor, será el día	1760 D
Cuando vayando vuelven	1720 2D
Dando a la playa	1744 2D

Dando al aire mas aliento	1735 D 1737
De amor exceso amante	1738
De amor la oficina	1737
De Belén las pastoras	1753
De Belén los carpinteros	1735 D
De Belén los oficiales	1738 D
De Belén los pastorcillos	1757 D 1755
De la nube fecunda	1737
De laja el prodigiosa	1749
De nuevo la aurora	1747
Deja que esas flechas	1746
Del fenix del cielo	1760 D
Del primer hombre	1758 D
Del universal presidio	1745 D
Delicioso clavel	1740
Desda Málaga esta noche	1737
Deseando cantar juntos	1743 D
Dígame, dígame	1737 D
Digo que no he de cantarla	1750 2D 1766
Diluvios de gracias	1735 D
Dirás plausibles	1740
Discretos sabios reyes	1763
Divina luz que ilustras	1764
Dos astrólogos	1740 D
Dos pastorcillos soldados	1752
Dos zagalas de Belén	1756
Dulce prenda del cielo	1758
Dulces teorbas	1737
Ea! Anfriso alegre	1752
Echo al aire un mar de luces	1748 D 1749 1766
El comilón honrado	1744 D
El consejo de Belén	1760 D
El herrador de Belén	1736
El retrato del Niño	1743 D
Electa para el bién	1745
En agua y en tierra	1737 D
En Belén en un pesebre	1764
En Belén los bordadores	1743 D
En círculo abreviado	1737
En el Aranjuez del mundo	1737 D
En el centro feliz	1759
En el claro cristal	1741
En el día del Señor	1735 D 1737
En el portal han entrado	1753
En esas aras	1747
En esa dulce hoguera	1752
En esta sacra mesa	1756
En las aras en quien admiramos	1733 D
En las ardientes alas	1737
En purezas y gracias	1749

En tanto que los zagales	1742 D
En tierra y en abismo	1755 D
Engañada mujer	1764
Enojado con el mundo	1749
Es el poder del hombre	1739
Es inmitable Dios omnipotente	1759 D
Es María tan pura	1763 D
Esa cumbre excelente	1748
Escóndanse rendidos	1737
Escuchad moradores del orbe	1751
Esta es aquella mesa	1756
Esta noche al Niño hermoso	1758 D
Esta noche al portal vienen	1737 D
Esta noche con gracejo	1741 D
Esta noche es nochebuena	1759 D
Esta noche lo Neglillo	1753
Eterno el dia	1733
Exceso es del amor	1757
Fábrica soberana	1757
Feliz el alma ansiosa	1745
Festivas zagalas	1745 D
Flores cogiendo va una pastorcilla	1733
Fogosa inteligencia	1737 D
Fuego, fuego	1741 D
Fuera, fuera que a Belén	1756 D 1760
Gire la bélica voz	1742
Gozosa el alma	1747
Gracia y naturaleza	1759 D
Graciosa y célebre	1737
Guapo ha de ser el tonillo	1755 D
Guerra pública el día	1744 2D 1768
Ha de haber jácara buena	1747
Ha de haber tonada	1736
Ha de la informe mansión	1759 D
Ha de Nembroth el barbaro edifcio	1740 D
Hacer quiere una comedia	1749 D
Haciendo fiel seña	1738
Haga a Leva la señal	1742
Haga salva canora	1750
Hagan armoniosa salve	1734 D 1745
Háganle salva liras armoniosas	1744 2D 1768
Hala, hala, que el cielo	1748 D 1755
Hala, hala, que el cielo	1756
Has visto Gila de esa luz	1743 D
Hasta aquí Dios amante	1741 D
Hasta cuando en el centro	1766
Helmana Flancisca	1743 D
Hermosa Ruth por serlo	1760 D
Hermoso imán mío	1766
Hola chiquillo	1747

Hola Jau	1751
Hola, hola, pastorcillos	1741
Hola, pastorcillos	1741
Hola pastores, que sonoro acento	1755 D 1757
Hombres prevenid puro	1758 D
Hoy canción traemos	1744
Hoy en un cielo nuevo	1755
Hoy entre la blancura	1757
Huya infiel serpiente	1744 D 1746
Huyan las sombras	1750 D
Huyendo la ruina	1740
Inefable portento	1766
Inmenso Dios	1754
Jácara de fandanguillo	1734
Jacarilla en campana	1757
Jardinera serpiente	1764
Jerusalén eleva	1755 D
Jesus! Jesus! María, y José	1763
La abejuela misteriosa	1758
La armonía de las aves	1739
La ciudad que en Pathmos vió	1750 D
La divina pastora	1766
La dulzura mayor	1748
La escala que vió Jacob	1734 D
La fiera en el monte	1739
La gloria se admire	1734
La humana Babilonia	1747
La más graciosa nave	1741 D
La naturaleza humana	1757 D
La noche se ostenta	1752
La Pastora Jileta	1751
La salva le hagamos	1744 D
La tonadilla graciosa	1747
La zagaleja Mirtila	1754 D 1769
Labrador divino	1749
Labrador oficioso deja	1741 2D
Las aves acordes	1756
Las dulces Filomenas	1743 D
Las gitanas bulliciosas	1750 D
Las hojas se mueven	1754
Las tiernas pastorcillas	1752 D
Las zagalas de Belén	1752 D
Las zagalas de la corte	1746 D
Linea señaló Dios	1749
Liras plausibles	1740
Llego paloma	1758
Llegando a la Troxes	1741
Llenando de alegrías	1744
Llévame los ojos	1738 2D 1744
Logras el valle	1749

Los chiquillos de Belén	1755 D
Los gallegos enfadados	1755 D 1757
Los marineros de flota	1739 D
Los muchachuelos del coro	1763 D
Los orbes celestiales	1754 D 1768
Los pájaros, los troncos	1737
Los pastores de Belén	1735 D
Los pastores de Belén	1735
Los plateros de Belén	1755 D
Los zagales a Fileno	1744 D
Mano a mano y sin pandero	1733 D
Marinerillo	1739
Marinero que surcas	1737
Mil veces sea bendito	1760 D
Milagro admiración	1751
Mirando humano al Niño	1744 D
Montados en sus esdrújulos	1738 D
Montes de Palestina	1754 D 1769
Montes tencdme envidia	1743 2D
Montes y riscos	1763
Muchachas al baile	1748 2D 1766
Muestra zéfiro amante	1750
Nevado alberque de un amor bizarro	1742 D
Niño agraciado	1735
Noticia Bartolo	1747
Nueva armonía	1749 D
Nuevo Balsaín le ofrece	1748 2D 1766
Oh! bienaventurada	1738 D
Oh! Dios, oh pan!	1764
Oh! fogoso volcán	1754
Oh! pan sacramentado	1753
Oh! que bien que suspenden	1756
Oh! que festivo placer	1758
Oh! que halagueña canción	1758
Oí Señor soberano	1749
Oí a ese corderito	1744
Oí en un cielo nuevo	1755
Oí tres baterías	1747 D 1746
Oí tres Reyes juntos	1749 D 1758
Oiga bella Niña	1745
Oiga Señor mío	1745 D
Oigan los campos de Booz	1760 D
Oigan que una peregrina	1755 D
Oigan una tonadilla	1756
Operarios a segar	1739
Oyendo un pajarote	1736 D
Oyenos la fina canción	1744 D
Oyes Hipólito	1736 2D
Pajarito soy con alma	1748
Para aplaudir al Señor	1739

Para celebrar la noche	1744 D
Para divertir al Niño	1750 D
Para hacer burla del diablo	1752 D
Para reclutar soldados	1745 D
Pastorela, pastores	1763
Pastorelica de bella invención	1751 D 1750
Pastorelilla aquí	1747
Pastores a un lado	1749
Pastores de Belén	1753
Pastores volad	1759 D 1760
Pastores y pastoras	1766
Pax di orbe	1751
Pensativa una pastora	1758 D
Per Maria Gratia plena	1753
Peregrinas al portal	1747
Piedad inmenso Dios	1756
Por aquel horizonte	1759
Por las calles buscando	1738 D
Por más que soberbio	1737
Por no faltar a la moda	1740 D
Por una deuda en prisiones	1742 D
Porque dichas del cielo	1751
Porque en la entrada festiva	1760 D
Predicó en Belén el cura	1727
Preste vuelos amor	1738
Prisioneros alentad	1736 D
Prosigue acorde lira	1720
Pues a navegar empieza Dios	1733 D
Pues en ese panal	1737
Pues está callando Bato	1733 D
Pues eterno el día	1733 2D 1738
Pues que Ruth a los campos	1760 D
Pues quien el ser nos libra	1764
Pues ya la serpiente	1740 D
Puesto que antaño gusto	1758 D
Pulcra Ester privilegiada	1765
Que alegre caminas	1744 D
Que alegría	1743 2D
Que armoniosa consonancia	1733 D 1735
Que asombro! Que maravilla!	1755 D
Que asombro zagales	1745 D
Que azucena	1745
Que bien abejuelas	1738
Que embarcación la playa	1745
Que es esto amor que veo!	1758 D
Que es esto cielos	1750 2D 1763
Que es lo que traes Silvia	1746 D
Que habreis primero vos	1741 D
Que halagueña canción!	1758
Que le diremos	1750

Que milagro, que portento	1737
Que misterio	1742
Que misterioso asombro	1744 D 1746
Que ráfaga de luz	1766
Que tempestad los orbes	1744 D
Que temprano bien mío	1748 D
Querubes del trono	1750
Quien me dirá como sabré	1733 2D
Quien me dirá con primor	1742
Rayando el alba	1746
Recoged las velas	1738 D
Renazcan los campos	1757
Reparad Zagales	1749 D 1750
Resonando a Isaías	1735 D
Respira Adán	1753
Respira sin temor naturaleza	1750 D
Resuenen estruendos	1734
Resuenen los ecos	1737
Sabia extensión	1746
Sabiendo que en noche buena	1738 D
Sagrada devoción	1757 D 1758
Saluden al alba	1741 D
Salve oh! Señor augusto	1751
Seguidillas muchachos	1759 D
Señor, que llanto es éste	1763
Señora parida yo soy un pastor	1763
Serafines que en el trono	1749
Serranillas a bailar	1739 D
Serranillas esta noche	1746 D
Si a nosotros se ha dado el hijo	1734 D
Si alabarte solicito	1750
Si para darme ese pan	1736 D 1737
Si por la primera culpa	1763 D
Siendo influjo el ardor	1740 D 1739
Siendo las obras	1736 D
Siendo pastor de fama	1745 D
Siguiendo los giros	1741 2D
Silva culebra infernal	1743 D
Silvio soy, músico antiguo	1739 D
Sol es María, que con luz ardiente	1765
Suspende ya los vuelos	1748
Toda de luces	1756
Todo confusión el Mundo	1759 D
Todo mortal constante	1760
Todo viene de vos	1758
Toquen los clarines	1752 D
Toribio con sus zagales	1759 D
Toribio, noble asturiano	1751
Toribión un Asturiano	1740 D
Tortolilla que amorosa	1737 D 1739

Tremolen sus banderas	1735 D 1737
Tres campeones de oriente	1736
Triste lamenta Israel	1738 D
Un cojo a ver a Dios niño	1766
Un crítico y un pastor	1737 D
Un danzante mi Niño	1754 D 1769
Un festín soberano	1742 D
Un gallardo portugués	1754 D 1769
Un grano misterioso	1759
Un maestro de capilla	1763
Un pajarero contento	1751
Un pastor muy Jacarero	1760 D
Un pastorcillo italiano	1749 D
Un rayo divino	1733 2D 1737
Un siciliano festivo	1754 D 1769
Un sobrio y un comilón	1739 D
Un zagalillo	1755 D
Una pastorcilla amante	1757 D 1755
Unas lavanderas vienen	1742 D
Una señora de manto	1734 D
Vamo calendita	1740
Vamos aprisa pastores	1756
Vamos claros mi Niño	1748 2D 1766
Vamos corriendo a buscar	1737
Vamos culendita	1740
Vamos, vamos pastorcillos	1740 D
Vaya de jácara	1748 D 1741
Vaya de parabienes	1737 D
Vaya de placer	1734 D
Vaya de tonadilla	1742 D
Vaya de tonadilla	1756
Vaya, vaya jacarilla	1759 D
Ven, nuevo Gedeón	1743
Venga incendio soberano	1737 2D
Venga tonadilla venga	1759 D
Vengan hoy al combate	1757
Vengan los pastorcillos	1754 D 1769
Venid al aplauso	1733 2D
Vesubio Soberano	1748
Viendo el Niño	1743 D
Viendo que Gil hizo raya	1745 D
Viendo que las novedades	1736
Viendo un seise a dos zagales	1750 D
Viniendo a Belén los reyes	1738 D
Violines rompió a nombre	1729
Volver al Niño monarca	1738
Vuele a ese incendio	1740
Ya anticipo la alegre primavera	1758 D
Ya llegando Señor	1747
Ya, oh gran naturaleza	1757 D

Ya que el Niño hermoso	1757 D 1755
Yo soy aquel furor	1757
Yo y dos brutos esta noche	1740 D
Zagales, como una pascua me vengo	1744 D
Zagales corred	1753
Zagales venid	1741 D 1740
Zas, jacarilla en campaña	1755

APPENDIX F

LIST OF THE VILLANCICOS SELECTED FOR THIS BOOK[1]

	Title	Date	Voices	Type	Occasion[2]	Instruments
1.	Pues eterno el día	1733	4		IMC	violins, oboe
2.	A Belén caminad pastorcillos	1736	2	Cantada	Xmas	violins
3.	Ay, que alegre festivo	1736	4		B.Sac.	violins
4.	El herrador de Belén	1736	5		Xmas	
5.	Prisioneros alentad	1736	8		Xmas	violins
6.	Vamos corriendo a buscar	1736	4		B.Sac.	violin
7.	Montados en sus esdrújulos	1738	2		Xmas	bajoncillos
8.	Recoged las velas	1738	8	Calenda	IMC	violins
9.	Triste lamenta Israel	1738	8	Calenda	Xmas	violins
10.	Corriendo Zagales	1740	5	Vizcaíno	Xmas	violins, oboes
11.	Cuando vayando vuelven	1740	4		B.Sac.	violins
12.	Delicioso clavel	1740	2	Cantada	IMC	violin, transverse flute
13.	Huyendo la ruina	1740	8	Calenda	B. Sac.	violins
14.	Vamos culendita	1740	3	De Negros	Xmas	violin
15.	Vamos culendita	1742	6	Tonadilla	Xmas	bajoncillos

[1] All of the villancicos have continuo; therefore, only the non-continuo instruments have been listed. The type of villancicos and the occasion in which they were performed are specified in the manuscripts.

[2] Immaculate Conception—IMC
Christmas—Xmas
Blessed Sacrament—B.Sac.

143

No.	Title	Year	No.	Genre	Occasion	Instrumentation
16.	Helmana Flancica	1743	6	De Negros	Xmas	bajoncillos
17.	Oiga Señor mío	1745	2		Xmas	bajoncillos, recorder
18.	A Belén pastorcillas	1749	7	Tonadilla	Xmas	violins, trompas
19.	Asi, al chocorrotiya	1749	5	De Negros	Xmas	violins, transverse flute, bajoncillos,bajón
20.	Hacer quiere una comedia	1749	4		Xmas	violins
21.	Reparad Zagales	1749	7	De Reyes	Xmas	violin, oboe, clarines
22.	Seguidillas muchachos	1749	7	Tonadilla	Xmas	violins
23.	Digo que noche de cantarla	1750	5	Jácara	Xmas	violins
24.	Para divertir al Niño	1750	7	Tonadilla	Xmas	violins, trompas
25.	Ea, Ea Anfiso alegre	1752	7	Tonadilla	Xmas	violins
26.	Las tiernas pastorcillas	1752	7	Pastorela	Xmas	violins, trompas
27.	Las zagalas de Belén	1752	8	Tonadilla	Xmas	violins, trompas
28.	Toquen los clarines	1752	8	Jácara	Xmas	violins, clarines
29.	Zagales corred	1753	8	Calenda	Xmas	violins, clarines, oboe, trompas
30.	Alados celestiales	1754	7	Calenda	B.Sac.	violins, trompas, oboe, clarines
31.	Batillo con su mujer	1754	2	Pastorela	Xmas	violins, trompas
32.	Las hojas se mueven	1754	4		B.Sac.	violins, clarines, trompas
33.	Un danzante mi Niño	1754	1		Xmas	violins, transverse flute, oboe
34.	Un siciliano festivo	1754	7	Siciliano	Xmas	violins, trompas
35.	Bato y Pascuala contentos	1755	8	Tonadilla	Xmas	violins, piccolo
36.	Los gallegos enfadados	1755	6		Xmas	violins, oboes, chirimía
37.	Los plateros de Belén	1755	8		Xmas	violins, trompas
38.	Las aves acordes	1756	8		B. Sac.	violins, trompas, recorder, oboe
39.	Ya que el Niño hermoso	1757	5	Pastorela	Xmas	violins, trompas
40.	Abandonados cautivos	1758	8	Calenda	Xmas	violins, transverse flute, trompas
41.	Oh! que halagueña canción	1758	2	Cantada	Xmas	violins, trompas
42.	Esta noche es nochebuena	1759	7	Tonadilla	Xmas	violins, transverse flute
43.	Un gallardo portugués	1759	7	Portugues	Xmas	violins

44.	Vaya, vaya jacarilla	1759	4	Jácara	Xmas	violins, transverse flute
45.	Cerrando la mogiganga	1760	8		Xmas	violins, chirimía, clarines
46.	Porque en la entrada festiva	1760	4		Xmas	violins
47.	Un pastor muy jacarero	1760	7	Jácara	Xmas	violins, recorder

APPENDIX G

TEXT OF THE FIVE VILLANCICOS TRANSCRIBED IN PART TWO

A BELÉN CAMINAD PASTORCILLOS

Introducción
A Belén caminad pastorcillos
que hay dos maravillas
pues recreo comun son de todos
Jesus y María

Recitative
Dulces ternezas que el amor inflama
Finos cariños que el placer explica
entre Hijo y Madre con piadosa llama
la mas ardiente unión se especifica
pues uno a otro en fiel correspondencia
se aplauden el favor y la clemencia

Aria amorosa
Me complaces, te venero
Madre mia, mi señor
yo te busco, yo te quiero
recreándonos los dos

Me arrebata, se acredita
tanta gracia, tanto amor
gozo añade, hierros quita
Virgen pura eterno Dios

Recitative
Contempla de su Dios Madre tan pura
Fineza imponderable
Admire en María la escencial dulzura
la gracia mas amable
y en finas muestras al placer unidos
con los hombres se dan por entendidos
pues María les da su fruto amado
y el se mira por ellos humanado

Pastorela
Celebren pastores con júbilo igual
en Hijo y en Madre belleza y piedad
mostrando gozosos que esta en el Portal
en uno y en otro la gloria y la paz

A Belén pastorcillos

A call to the sheperds to go to Belén to worship the virgin Mary and the Child

146

A BELÉN, A BELÉN PASTORCILLAS

Estribillo
A Belén, a Belén pastorcillas
Al portal, al portal zagalejas
porque haya juguete
que al Niño divierta
y la tonadilla
nacida le venga

Y Bato muchachas
A donde se queda
pues canto que espanto
un hato de ovejas
y hato por hato
mayor con buen rato
el hato son ellas

Que lindo simplote gentil no le deja
querer con nosotras que el Niño le atienda

Quien les ha dicho
las muy picoteras
que el Niño sabio
nacido a la tierra
no suplirá a un tonto
pues sufre dos bestias

tiene razón vaya la tonadilla
tengo razón y chitón y chitón que comienza

Que aires son los que te traen
dime dulce amada Prenda
a tomar puerto en el mundo
desde el mar de tus finezas
hazte a la vela ay Niño mío
porque te esperan de ingratitudes
en tan mal puerto muchas tormentas
pues las muchachas soportan
a decir conmigo vuelvan

Copla 1
Desde el golfo de tus glorias
el amor te lisongea
a que con aura apacible
dejes cielo y tomes tierra

147

Respuesta 1
Hazte a la vela ay Niño mío
antes que vean como te impelen
notos que braman
vientos que sientas

Copla 2
Cuando las serenidades
tienen el mar de tus clemencias
quieres padecer borrascas
en el puerto a que te entregas

Respuesta 2
Hazte a la vela ay Niño mío
sino es que quieras que sepa el mundo
que apenas naces
naces apenas

Copla 3
Viendo playa tan hinchada
de vanidad y soberbia
en sus profusiones locas
le dejaras por loquera

Respuesta 3
Hazte a la vela ay Niño mío
porque da señas este mal mundo
que apenas naces
naces apenas

Copla 4
Se que en el puerto del mundo
padeceras cruel tormenta
y sera con pasión verte
verte que pierdas la vida en ella

Respuesta 4
Hazte a la vela ay Niño mío
bien que se advierta que tu amor quiere
con tempestades
de ser tronera

A Belén, a Belén pastorcillas

The sheperdesses go to Belén to play and sing with the Child. The Child is compared to a sailor debarking in this stormy world. He is beseeched to sail away from a future of ingratitudes.

LAS ZAGALAS de BELÉN

Introduction
La Zagalas de Belén
traen sus tijeretillas
para divertir al Niño
con una gran Tonadilla

Estribillo
Cantemos alegres
gustosas y unidas
a este corderito
que es nuestra alegría

Empiece Pascuala
y todas repitan
la canción gustosa
de nuestra inventive

Copla 1
Cordero del alma
que vienes de arriba
a sacrificarte
por darnos la vida

Copla 2
Al redil te vienes
y tal lo iluminas
que siendo de noche
parece que es día

Copla 3
Corderito eres
y Pastor te admiran
los que te conocen
fieles ovejitas

Copla 4
Y pues tu fineza
nuestro obsequio excita
humilde las gracias
te damos rendidas

Respuesta[*]

Ven ven
y suenen que suenen las tijeretillas
ven aprisita
ven ven
ven aprisita
y suenen que suenen las tijeretillas
chas chas chas chas de la prisa
chas chas chas de la prisa de la prisa

Las zagalas de Belén

The young girls of Belén sing their pastoral tunes to the Child. The infant Jesus is viewed as a sacrificial lamb that comes from Heaven to redeem us with his life. The composition uses onomatopoeic shearing sounds.

---

[*] The respuesta is sung after each one of the *coplas*.

ALADOS CELESTIALES

Recitative
Alados celestiales querubines
aclamad por el orbe y sus confines
la fineza mayor de heroico anhelo
pues la tierra se adorna nuevo cielo

Aria
Cantad fieles querubes
alegres y sonoros
cantad sobre las nubes
cantad en dulces coros
cantad fineza la mayor
al tierno Dios de amores
cantadle con primores
la palma la victoria
que a tan gustosa gloria
nos brinda con su amor

Alados celestiales

The cherubs are beseeched to descend to Earth to sing laudatory chants to the Lord of love.

AVES ACORDES

Entrada
Las aves acordes
canoros los vientos
en dulces cadencias
alternen a un tiempo

Sagrados motetes
al gran Sacramento
repitiendo unidos
sonoros los ecos

Que duerme mi amado ce-ce
que duerme mi Dueño ce-ce
descansa mi vida ce-ce
descansa mi cielo ce-ce

Recitative
En esa azul campaña dilatada
los plumados vajeles matizados
de tanto bien la gloria duplicada
celebren con acentos acordados
porque resuene al viento
la gracia singular del Sacramento

Aria
La tortola suave
la amante Filomena
trine sonora y grave
cante sin susto y pena
al mas divino Pan

Porque al mirar ansiosa
el alma tanto amor
respira ya gozosa
y alienta su temor
con don tan celestial

Copla 5
Que aires son los que te traen
dime dulce amada prenda
a tomar puerto en el mundo
desde el mar de tus finezas

Respuesta 5
Hazte a la vela ay Niño mío
porque te esperan de ingratitudes
en tan mal puerto
muchas tormentas

Aves acordes

Birds and doves trill and coo their lullabies to the Child.

152

BIBLIOGRAPHY

BIBLIOGRAPHY

Albong, Juan Luis. *Historia de la Literature Española*. Vols. 2 and 3. Madrid: Editorial Gredos, S.A., 1972.

Alonso, Dámaso. "Cancioncillas 'de amigos' Mozárabes." *Revista de Filología Española* 33 (1949): 297-349.

Amador de los Ríos, José. *Obras de Don Iñigo Lopez de Mendoza, Marqués de Santillana*. Madrid: n.p. 1852.

Anglés, Higinio, ed. *La Música en la Corte de los Reyes Católicos: Polifonía religiosa. Monumentos de la Música Española* 1. Madrid: Consejo Superior de Investigaciones Científicas, 1941.

——————, ed. *La Música en la Corte de los Reyes Católicos: Polifonía Profana*. Monumentos de la Música Española 5 and 10. Madrid: Consejo Superior de Investigaciones Científicas, 1947 and 1951.

—————— and Subirá, José, eds. *Catálogo musical de la Biblioteca Nacional de Madrid*. 3 vols. Barcelona: Instituto Español de Investigaciones Científicas, 1946.

Aretz, Isabel. "Cantos Navideños en el Folklore Venezolano." *Boletín Interamericano de Música*. Part 1 (July 1965): 3-14. Part 2 (May 1969): 3-20.

Arnold, F.T. *The Art of Accompaniment from a Thorough-Bass*. London: Oxford University Press, 1931.

Artero, José. "Oposiciones al Magisterio de Capilla en España durante el Siglo XVIII." *Anuario Musical* 2 (1947): 191-202.

Asenjo Barbieri, Francisco, ed. *Cancionero musical de los siglos XV y XVI*. Buenos Aires: Editorial Schapire, 1949.

Ayestaran, Lauro. "El Barroco Musical Hispanoamericano." *Yearbook of the Inter-American Institute for Musical Research* 1 (1965): 66-78.

Baines, Anthony. *European and American Musical Instruments*. New York: The Viking Press, Inc., 1966.

Bleiberg, Germán and Marias, Julian, ed. *Diccionario de Literatura Española*. Madrid: Revista de Occidente, 1964.

Boleas y Sintas, Miguel. *La Catedral de Málaga*. Málaga: Talleres de Imprenta de Arturo Gilabert, 1894.

Bukofzer, Manfred. *Music in the Baroque Era*. New York: W.W. Norton and Company, Inc., 1947.

Burns, Joseph A. "Malaga Cathedral Organs are Fine Specimen." *The Diapason* 55:12 (November 1960): 8-9.

Carriazo, J.M. *Cronica de los Reyes Católicos*. Madrid: 1927.

Carse, Adam. *The History of Orchestration*. New York: E.P. Dutton and Company, 1925.

————. *Musical Wind Instruments*. New York: Da Capo Press, 1965; Reprint ed., London: Macmillan, 1939.

————. *The Orchestra in the XVIII Century*. Cambridge: W. Heffer and Sons, Ltd., 1940.

Catalyne, Alice Ray. "Music of the Sixteenth to Eighteenth Centuries in the Cathedral of Puebla, Mexico." *Yearbook of the Inter-American Institute for Musical Research* 2 (1966).

Cerbellón de la Vera, Estaquio. *Diálogo armónico sobre el Teatre crítico universal en defense de la Música de los templos dedicado a las tres capillas reales de esta Corte las de su Majestad, señoras Descalzas y señoras de la Encarnación*. n.p., 1726.

Chase, Gilbert. "Juan del Encina: Poet and Musician." *Music and Letters* 20 (October 1939): 420-30.

————. *The Music of Spain*. New York: W.W. Norton and Company, Inc., 1959.

————. "Origins of the Lyrical Theater in Spain." *The Musical Quarterly* 25 (July 1939): 292-305.

Ciurczak, Peter. "The Trumpet in Baroque Opera: Its Use As Solo, Obligato, and Ensemble Instrument." Ph.D. Dissertation North Texas State University, 1974.

Civil, Francisco. "La música en la Catedral de Gerona durante el siglo XVII." *Anuario Musical* 15 (1960): 219-46.

Cotarelo y Mori, Emilio. *Colección de Entremeses, Loas, Bailes,Jácaras y Mojigangas desde fines del Siglo XVI a mediados del XVIII*. Madrid: Tipografía de la "Revista de archivos, bibliotecas y museos," 1911.

——————. *Orígines y establecimiento de la ópera en España*. Madrid: Tipografía de la "Revista de archivos, biblotecas y museos," 1911.

Davis, J.D., ed. *A Dictionary of Liturgy and Worship*. New York: The Macmillan Company, 1972.

Díaz Plaja, Fernando. *La vida española en el siglo XVII*. Barcelona: Editorial Alberto Martín, 1946.

Díaz Rengifo, Juan. *Arte poética española*. Barcelona: María Angela Maoti, 1759.

Diccionario de la Música Labor. 1954 ed. S.v. "Francés de Iribarren."

Donington, Robert. *The Instruments of Music*. 2nd ed. London: Methuen and Company, Ltd., 1962.

——————. *The Interpretation of Early Music*. London: Faber and Faber, Ltd., 1963.

Donostia, P. José Antonio de and Tomás, Juan. "Instruments de música popular española." *Anuario Musical* 2 (1947): 105-50.

Encyclopédie de la Musique et Dictionnaire du Conservatoire. Vol. IV, premiére partie. Paris: Librarie Delagrave, 1920. S.v. "Espagne," by Rafael Mitjana.

Eslava, Hilarión. *Breve memoria histórica de la música religiosa en España*. Madrid: Imprenta de Luis Beltrán, 1860.

Espinosa, C S. J., Sister Teresita. "Selected Unpublished Villancicos of Padre Fray Antonio Soler with Reference to the Cultural History of Eighteenth Century Spain." Ph.D. dissertation, University of Southern California, 1969.

Frenk Alatorre, Margit. "Glosas de tipo popular en la antigua lírica." *Nueva Revista de Filología Hispánica* 12 (1958): 301-34.

García Matos, M. "Instrumentos musicales folklóricos de España." *Anuario Musical* 9 (1954): 161-78.

Geiger, Albert. "Bausteine zur Geschichte des iberischen Vulgar= Villancico." *Zeitschrift fur Musikwissenschaft* 4 (November 1921): 65-93.

Gerhard, Mia I. *La Pastorela*. Assen, Holland: 1950.

Gradenwitz, Peter. "Mid-Eighteenth Century Transformation of Style." *Music and Letters* 18:3 (July 1937): 265-75.

Grebe, María Ester. "Introducción al estudio del villancico in Latinoamérica." *Revista Musical Chilena* 23 (April-June, 1969).

Grove's Dictionary of Music and Musicians. 1954 ed. S.G. "Anthem," by Edmund H. Fellows.

—————, 1954 ed. S.v. "Cantata," by Edward J. Dent.

Hamilton, Mary Deal. *Music in Eighteenth Century Spain.* Princeton, N.J.: Princeton University Press, 1958.

Jacobs, Charles. *Tempo, Notation in Renaisance Spain.* Musicological Studies, No. 8. New York: Institute of Medieval Music, 1953.

Kastner, Santiago M. *Contribución al estudio de la música española y portuguesa.* Lisbon: Editorial Atica, Iltda., 1941.

—————. "La música en la Catedral de Badajoz (años 1654-1764)." *Anuario Musical* 18 (1963): 223-238.

—————. *Sette Pezzi per Arpa dei secoli XVII e XVIII tratti da antichi manuscritti spagnoli e portoghesi.* Milano: Edizioni Luvini Zerboni, 1972.

Lees-Milne, James. *Baroque in Spain and Portugal.* London: B.T. Batsford, Ltd., 1960.

The Liber Usualis. Ed. by the Benedictines of Solesmes. Tournai: Desclee and Co., 1934.

Llordén, Andrés P., O.S.A. "Inventario musical de 1770 en la Catedral de Málaga." *Anuario Musical* 24 (1970): 237-46.

—————. "Notas de los maestros organeros que trabajaron en Málaga." *Anuario Musical* 13 (1958): 167-93.

—————. "Notas históricas de los maestros de capilla en la Catedral de Málaga (1641-1799)." *Anuario Musical* 19 (1966): 71-93.

—————. "Notas históricas de los maestros organistas de la Catedral de Málaga (1585-1799)." *Anuario Musical* 20 (1967): 105-160.

—————. "Notas históricas de los maestros organistas de la Catedral de Málaga (1585-1799)." *Anuario Musical* 22 (1969): 145-70.

—————. "Notas históricas de los maestros organistas de la Catedral de Málaga (1584-1799)." Part Two. *Anuario Musical* 23 (1970): 158-59.

Lopez Calo, José. "Fray José de Baquedano, (1681-1711) maestro de capilla de la Catedral de Santiago." *Anuario Musical* 10 (1955): 191-216.

——————. *La música en la Catedral de Granada en el siglo XVI.* Granada: Fundación Rodriguez Acosta, 1963.

Lorente, Andrés. *El porque de la música.* Alcalá de Henares: Imprenta de Nicolas de Xamares, 1762.

Madurell, José María. "Documentos para la historia de maestros de capilla, infantes de coro, maestros de música y danza y ministriles en Barcelona (siglos XIV-XVIII)." *Anuario Musical* 3 (1948): 214-34.

——————. "Documentos para la historia de maestros de capilla, organistas, órganos, organeros, músicos e instrumentos (siglos XIV-XVIII." *Anuario Musical* 4 (1949): 193-220.

Mayer-Serra, Otto. *Música y músicos de Latinoamérica.* Mexico City: Editorial Atlanta, 1947.

Mazzei, Angel. *Historia de la Literatura Española.* Buenos Aires: Editorial Ciordia, S.R.L., 1958.

Menéndez Pidal, Ramón. *Estudios literarios.* Mexico: Espasa-Calpe Argentina, S.A., 1938.

——————. *The Spaniards in Their History.* Translated with a Prefatory Essay by Walter Starkie. New York: W.W. Norton, 1950.

Moll, Jaime. "Los Villancicos cantados en la Capilla Real a fines del siglo XVI y principios del siglo XVII." *Anuario Musical* 25 (1970): 81-96.

——————. "Un villancico de Morales y otro de Cáceres en el Cancionero español de Upsala." *Anuario Musical* 8 (1953): 167-9.

Die Musik in Geschichte und Gegenwart, 1958 ed. S.v. "Kantata: Die protestantishche Kirchen-kantate." by Georg Feder.

——————, 1966 ed. S.v. "Villancico," by Isabel Pope.

Narvaez, Luys de. *Los seys libros del Delphin de Musica.* Edited by Emilio Pujol. *Monumentos de la Música Española* 3. Barcelona: Consejo Superior de Investigationes Científicas, 1945.

Nasarre, Pablo. *Escuela música según la práctica moderna.* 2 vols. Saragoza: Talleres de Diego Larrumbe y Manuel Román, 1724 and 1723.

New Catholic Encyclopedia, 1967 ed. S.v. "Mendoza, Gonzalez de," by D.W. Lomax.

Newman, William S. *The Sonata in the Baroque Era.* Chapel Hill: University of North Carolina Press, 1963.

Pedrell, Felipe. *Cancionero Musical Popular Español.* 2 vols. Barcelona: A Boileau y Bernasconi, n.d.

──────────, ed. *Diccionario técnico de la música.* Barcelona: Imprenta de Victor Bendos, 1894.

──────────, ed. *Diccionario técnico de la música.* Supplement. Barcelona: Isidro Torres Oriol, n.d.

Pena, Joaquín and Anglés, Higinio, eds. *Diccionario de la música Labor.* 2 vols. Barcelona: Editorial Labor, S.A., 1954.

Pedra, Joaquín. "Maestros de Capilla del Real Colegio de Corpus Christi (1662-1822)." *Anuario Musical* 23 (1968): 61-127.

Pope, Isabel. "Musical and Metrical Form of the Villancico." *Annales musicologiques* 2 (1954): 189-214.

──────────. "The Musical Development and Form of the Spanish Villancico." *Papers of the American Musicological Society* (1940): 11-22.

Pujol, Francisco. "Clasificación de las canciones populares." *Anuario Musical* 1 (1946): 19-29.

Querol Gavaldá, Miguel. "El romance polifónico en el siglo XVII." *Anuario Musical* 10 (1955): 111-20.

──────────, ed. *Cancionero Musical de la Casa de Medinacelli. Monumentos de la Música Española,* 9. Barcelona: Consejo Superior de Investigaciones Científicas, 1950.

──────────, ed. *Música Barroca Española. Monumentos de la Música Española* 18 Barcelona: Consejo Superior de Investigaciones Científicas.

Reese, Gustave. *Music in the Renaissance.* New York: W.W. Norton, 1959.

Ribera, Julian. *Music in Ancient Arabia and Spain*. Translated and abridged by Eleanor Hague and Marion Seffingwell. California: Standard University Press, 1929.

Ripollés, Vicente. *El villancico i la cantata del siglo XVIII a Valéncia*. Barcelona: Institut de'Estudis Catalans, — Biblioteca Catalunya, 1935.

Roda, Cecilio de. "La música Profana en el Reinado de Carlos I." *Revista Musical de Bilbao*, 1912.

Russel, Eleanor Ann. "Villancicos and other Secular Polyphonic Music of Juan Vasquez: a courtly Tradition in Spain's Siglo del Oro." Ph.D. Dissertation, University of Southern California, 1970.

Salazar, Adolfo. "El Gran Siglo de la música española." *Revista musical chilena* 9:1 (April 1954): 14-28.

——————. "La música española en tiempos de Goya." *Revista de Occidente* (Madrid: December 1928): 336.

——————. "Poesía y música en las primeras formas." *Filosofía y Letras* 4 (1942): 287-349.

Sanchez Romeralo, Antonio. *El Villancico*. Madrid: Editorial Gredos, S.A., 1969.

St. Amour, Sister Mary Paulina. *A Study of the Villancico Up to Lope de Vega*. Washington, D.C.: The Catholic University of America, 1940.

Selva, José. *El arte en España durante los Borbones*. Barcelona: Editorial, Amaltea, S.S., 1943.

Smithers, Don L. *The Music and History of the Baroque Trumpet before 1721*. London: J.M. Dent and Sons, 1973.

Soler, Antonio, P. Fr. *Llave de la modulación y antiguedades de la música*. Madrid: Taller de Joaquín Ibarra, 1762.

Soriano, Fuertes, Mariano. *Historia de la Música Española*. Vols. 1 and 2 Madrid: Martin y Salazar, 1855. Vol. 3 Barcelona: Narciso Ramirez, 1866.

Squire, W. Barclay. *Catalogue of Printed Music Published between 1487 and 1800 Now in the British Museum*. London: Longmans and Company, 1912.

Starkie, Walter. *Spain, a Musician's Journey through Time and Space*. 2 vols. Geneva: Rene Kister, 1958.

Stevenson, Robert M. *Music in Mexico*. New York: Thomas Y. Crowell Company, 1952.

—————, *Renaissance and Baroque Musical Sources in the Americas*. Washington, D.C.: General Secretariat, Organization of American States, 1970.

—————. *Spanish Cathedral Music in the Golden Age*. Berkeley: University of California Press, 1961.

—————. *Spanish Music in the Age of Columbus*. The Hague: Martinus Nijhoff, 1960.

Subirá, José. *Historia de la Música Española e Hispanoamericana*. Madrid: Salvat editores, S.A., 1953.

—————. *Historia de la música teatral en España*. Barcelona: Editorial Labor, S.A., 1945.

—————. *La tonadilla escénica*. 3 vols. Madrid: Tipografía de Archivos, 1928.

—————. "Un manuscrito de principios del siglo XVIII." *Anuario Musical* 5, (1949): 181-91.

Tello, Francisco José León. *La Teoria Española de la Música en los Siglos XVII y XVIII*. Madrid: Consejo Superior de Investigaciones Científicas, 1974.

Torres y Martinez Bravo, José de. *Reglas de acompañar en órgano, clavicordi y harpa...* Madrid: En la Imprenta de Música, 1702 and 1736.

Trend, John Brande. *The Music of Spanish History to 1600*. Oxford: Oxford University Press, 1926.

—————. *A Picture of Modern Spain*. New York: Houghton Mifflin, 1921.

Vásquez, Juan. *Recopilación de Sonetos y Villancicos a quatro y a cinco*. Transcribed by Higinio Anglés. *Monumentos de la Música Española* 4. Barcelona: Consejo Superior de Investigaciones Científicas, 1946.

PART TWO

MUSIC TRANSCRIPTIONS OF
VILLANCICOS
BY JUAN FRANCÉS DE IRIBARREN

PART TWO

Table of Contents

Villancico Cantada a Dúo con Violines

al Nacimiento del Niño Redentor

"A Belén Caminad Pastorcillos"

Año 1736

Cantada a Dúo al Santo Nacimiento — Maestro Iribarren Año 1736

Introducción a Medio Aire

A — Be-lén ca-mi-nad pastorcillos

A — Be-lén ca-mi-nad pastorcillos

que hay dos ma-ra-vi-llas que hay dos ma-ra-vi — llas que hay dos ma ra vi

que hay dos ma-ra-vi-llas que hay dos ma-ra-vi — llas que hay dos ma ra vi

-llas   pues   re-cre-o   co-mun son de to-dos

-llas   pues   re-cre-o   co-mun son de to-dos Je-

Je-sus   y Ma-ri-   a   Je-sus   Je-sus

sus   y Ma-ri-   a   Je-sus   Je-

173

Recitativo

Tiple

Dul-ces ter-ne-zas que el a-mor in-fla-ma fi-nos ca-ri-ños

Acompañamiento

que el pla-cer ex-pli-ca en-te Hi-jo y Ma-dre con pia-do-sa lla-ma la-más ar-dien-te u-

nion se es-pe-ci-fi-ca pues u-no_a o-tro en fiel co-rres-pon-den-cia a-

plau-den el fa-vor y la cle-men-cia

178

_-do-nos re-cre-an-do-nos los dos

_-do-nos re-cre-an-do-nos los dos

Me com-pla- ces

te ve-

Ma- dre mi- a

ne- ro

mi Se- ñor

yo_ te_ bus-co

yo_ te_

180

181

tan-ta gra- cia   go- zo_a-

tan-to_a_mor

ña-de   Vir-gen pu-ra_e-ter-no

hie- rros qui-ta   Vir-gen pu-ra_e-ter-no

Dios Vir-gen pu-ra e-ter-no Dios Vir-gen pu-ra

Dios Vir-gen pu-ra e-ter-no Dios Vir-gen pu-ra

e- ter- no Dios

e- ter- no. Dios

Recitativo a Duo

Tiple: Con-tem-pla de su Dios Ma-dre tan pu-ra fi-ne-za im-pon-de-ra-ble

Alto: mi-ra en Ma-

(130)

y en fi-nas mues-tras al pla-cer u-ni-dos con los

ri-a la e-sen-cial dul-zu-ra la gra-cia mas a-ma-ble y en fi-nas mues-tras al pla-cer u-ni-dos con los

(135)

hom-bres se dan por en-ten-di-dos pues Ma-ri-a les da su fru-to a-ma-do y el se mi-ra por e-llos hu-ma-

hom-bres se dan por en-ten-di-dos pues Ma-ri-a les da su fru-to a-ma-do y el se mi-ra por e-llos hu-ma-

na-__ do

na-__ do

186

Pastorela a Duo

Ce-le-bren pas-to-res con ju-bi-lo i

Ce-le-bren pas-to-res con ju-bi-lo i

gual en Hi- jo y en Ma-dre be-lle- za y pie-dad en Hi-___ jo y en Ma-dre be

gual en Hi-, jo y en Ma- dre be-lle- za y pie-dad en

lle-za y pie-dad be-lle-za be-lle-za y pie-dad

Hi- jo y en Ma-dre be-lle-za y pie-dad y pie-dad

mos-tran-do go-zo-sos que_es-ta_en el Por-tal en u_no y en o-_tro la glo-ria y la

mos-tran-do go-zo-sos que_es-ta_en el Por-tal en u_no y en o-_tro la glo-ria y la

paz en u-no y en o-tro la glo-ria y la paz la glo-ria y la paz la glo- ria y la

paz en u-no y en o-tro la glo-ria y la paz la glo- ria la glo-ria y la

paz

paz

Ce-le- bren pas-to-_res con ju-_bi-lo,i-gual   en u-_no y,en o-tro la glo-ria,y la

Ce-le- bren pas-to-res con ju-bi-la,i-gual   en u-_no y,en o-tro la

paz la paz la glo——— ria y) la glo-ria y la paz   la   glo——ria y la

glo——ria y la paz   la glo-ria y) la glo-ria y la paz   la

paz   y la paz   en u——no y en o-tro la glo-ria y la paz

glo—ria y) la paz   en u——no y en o——tro la glo-ria y la paz

tasto solo

191

la glo-ria y la paz

la glo-_____ria y la, paz

Villancico de Tonadilla de

Navidad con Violines y Trompas

" A Belén Pastorcillos"

Año 1749

* Indicated as 3° on the last page of the manuscript.

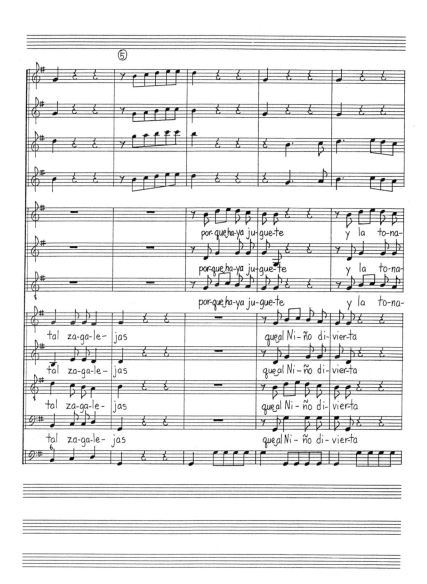

por-que ha-ya ju-gue-te   y la to-na-

por-que ha-ya ju-gue-te   y la to-na-

por-que ha-ya ju-gue-te   y la to-na-

tal za-ga-le- jas   que al Ni-ño di-vier-ta

tal za-ga-le- jas   que al Ni-ño di-vier-ta

tal za-ga-le- jas   que al Ni-ño di-vier-ta

tal za-ga-le- jas   que al Ni-ño di-vier-ta

di-lla

di-lla

di-lla / solo / y Ba-to mu-cha-chas / a don-de se

na-ci-da le ven-ga

na-ci-da le ven-ga

na-ci-da le ven-ga

na-ci-da le ven-ga

que-da   pues can-to que es-pan-to   un ha-to de o-ve- jas   y

ha- to por ha - to   ma-yor con buen ra- to   el ha- to son e-

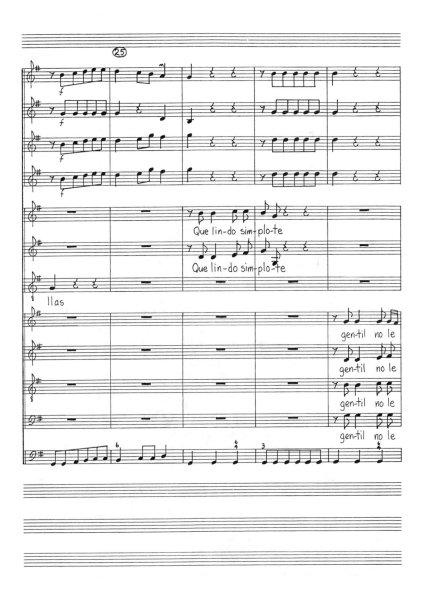

Que lin-do sim-plo-te

Que lin-do sim-plo-te

llas

gen-til no le

gen-til no le

gen-til no le

gen-til no le

que-rer con no-so-tras que el Ni-ño le a-tien-da

que-rer con no-so-tras que el Ni-ño le a tien-da

solo
Quien les ha di-

de-ja que-rer con no-so-tras que el Ni-ño le a-tien-da

de-ja que-rer con no-so-tras que el Ni-ño le a-tien-da

de-ja que-rer con no-so-tras que el Ni-ño le a-tien-da

de-ja que-rer con no-so-tras que el Ni-ño le a-tien-da

cho   las muy pi-co-te-   ras   queel Ni-ño sa- bio   na

ci - do a la tie - rra   no su - pli - ra un ton - to   pues su - fre dos bes-

tie-ne ra-zón   Va-ya la to-na

tie-ne ra-zón   Va-ya la to-na-

tias

Va-ya   Va-ya la to-na-

Va-ya   Va-ya la to-na-

Va-ya   Va-ya la to-na-

Va-ya   Va-ya la to-na-

di-lla
di-lla
solo
ten-go ra-zón   y chi-ton   y chi-ton que co-mien-
di-lla
di-lla
di-lla
di-lla

za

tonadilla

que ai-res son los que te

205

tra-en di-me dul-ce a-ma-da Pren-da

a to-

mar puer-toen el mun-do des de el mar de tus fi- ne- zas

207

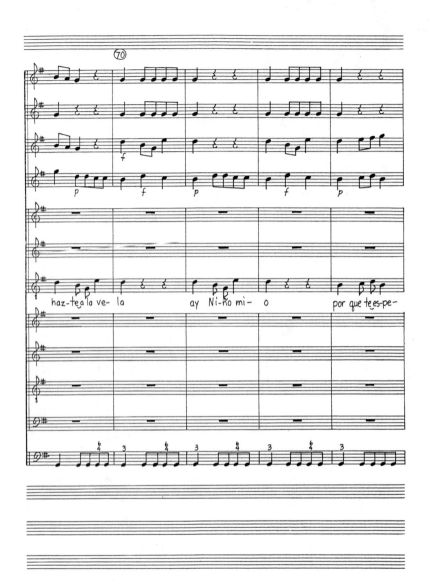

haz-te a la ve- la   ay Ni-ño mi- o   por que te es-pe-

ran   de jn-gra-ti-tu- des   en tan mal puer- to

209

mu-chas tor-men-tas

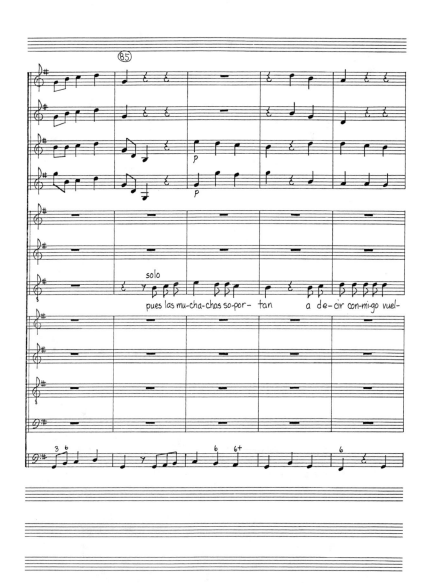

pues las mu-cha-chas so-por- tan   a de-cir con-mi-go vuel-

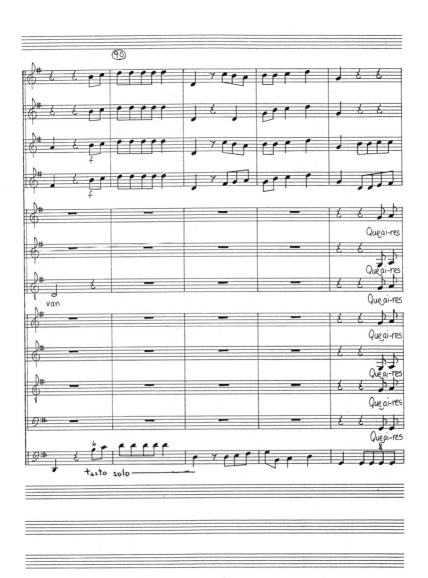

son los que te tra-en di-me dul-ce_a-ma-da Pren-da

son los que te tra-en di-me dul-ce_a-ma-da Pren-da

son los que te tra-en di-me dul-ce_a-ma-da Pren-da

son los que te tra-en di-me dul-ce_a-ma-da Pren-da

son los que te tra-en di-me dul-ce_a-ma-da Pren-da

son los que te tra-en di-me dul-ce_a-ma-da Pren-da

son los que te tra-en di-me dul-ce_a-ma-da Pren-da

a to-mar puer-to en el mun-do des de el mar de tus fi-ne- zas

a to-mar puer-to en el mun-do des de el mar de tus fi-ne- zas

a to-mar puer-to en el mun-do des de el mar de tus fi- ne-zas

a to-mar puer-to en el mun-do des de el mar de tus fi-ne- zas

a to-mar puer-to en el mun-do des de el mar de tus fi-ne- zas

a to-mar puer-to en el mun-do des de el mar de tus fi-ne- zas

a to-mar puer-to en el mun-do des de el mar de tus fi-ne- zas

haz-te̯a la ve - la   ay Ni-ño mí - o

haz-te̯a la ve - la   ay Ni-ño mí - o

haz-te̯a la ve - la   ay Ni-ño mí - o

haz-te̯a la ve - la   ay Ni-ño mí - o

haz-te̯a la ve - la   ay Ni-ño mí - o

haz-te̯a la ve- la   ay Ni-ño mí - o

haz-te̯a la ve - la   ay Ni-ño mí - o

215

por-que te es-pe- ran   de in-gra-ti-tu- des   en tan mal puer-

216

Coplas

1a. Des de el gol - fo de tus glo - rias el a-

2a. Cuan-do las se-re-ni-da-des tiene el
3a. Vien-do pla-ya tan hin-cha-da de va-

4a. Se que en el puer-to del mun-do pa-de-

2. mar de tus cle-men-cias   quie-res pa-de-cer bo-
3. ni-dad y so-ber-bia   en sus pro-fu-sio-nes

4. ce-ras cruel tor-men-ta   y se-ra com-pa-sión

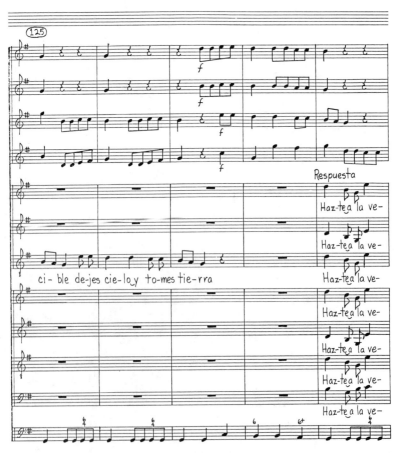

2. rras-cas en el puer-to_a que te_en-tre-gas   2a. Haz-te_a la ve-
3. lo-cas la de-ja-ras   por lo-que-ra   3a. Haz-te_a la ve-

4. ver-te que pier-das la vi-da_en e-lla   4a. Haz-te_a la ve-

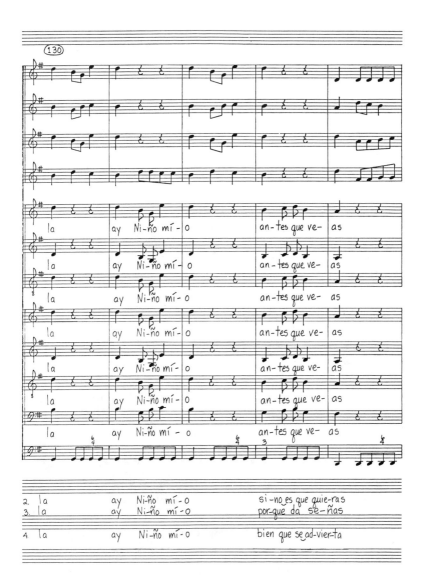

2. la   ay   Ni-ño mí - o   si-no_es que quie-ras
3. la   ay   Ni-ño mí - o   por-que da se-ñas

4. la   ay   Ni-ño mí - o   bien que se_ad-vier-ta

2. que se-pa el mun-do   que a-pe-nas na-ces   na-ces a-pe-
3. es-te mal mun-do   que a-pe-nas na-ces   na-ces a-pe-

4. que tu a-mor quie-re   con tem-pes-ta-des   de ser tro-ne-

2. nas.

3. nas.

4. ra.

223

225

Respuesta

ne-zas   Haz-te a la ve- la   ay Ni-ño mí-

ne-zas   Haz-te a la ve- la   ay Ni-ño mí-

ne-zas   Haz-te a la ve- la   ay Ni-ño mí-

ne-zas   Haz-te a la ve- la   ay Ni-ño mí-

ne-zas   Haz-te a la ve- la   ay Ni-ño mí-

ne-zas   Haz-te a la ve- la   ay Ni-ño mí-

ne-zas   Haz-te a la ve- la   ay Ni-ño mí-

o — por-que te_es-pe- ran de_in-gra-ti-tu- des

o — por-que te_es-pe- ran de_in-gra-ti-tu- des

o — por-que te_es-pe- ran de_in-gra-ti-tu- des

o — por-que te_es-pe- ran de_in-gra-ti-tu- des

o — por-que te_es-pe- ran de_in-gra-ti-tu- des

o — por-que te_es-pe- ran de_in-gra-ti-tu- des

o — por-que te_es-per ran de_in-gra-ti-tu- des

227

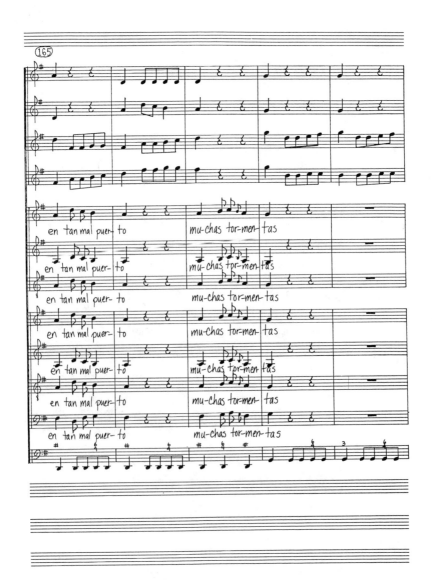

en tan mal puer- to   mu-chas tor-men- tas

en tan mal puer- to   mu-chas tor-men- tas

en tan mal puer- to   mu-chas tor-men- tas

en tan mal puer- to   mu-chas tor-men- tas

en tan mal puer- to   mu-chas tor-men- tas

en tan mal puer- to   mu-chas tor-men- tas

en tan mal puer- to   mu-chas tor-men- tas

229

Villancico de Tonadilla de Navidad

a 8 con Violines y Trompas

"Las Zagalas de Belén"

Año 1752

Introducción Arioso

Trompa 1ª
Trompa 2ª
Violín 1ª
Violín 2°

1 CORO
Tiple
Tiple
Alto
Tenor

2 CORO
Tiple — Las Za-ga-las de Be-lén
Alto — Las Za-ga-las de Be-lén
Tenor — Las Za-ga-las de Be-lén
Bajo — Las Za-ga-las de Be-lén
Acompañamiento

*Indicated as 6° on the last page of the manuscript.

tra-en sus ti - je-re- ti-llas   pa-ra di-ver-tir   al

tra-en sus ti - je-re-ti-llas   pa-ra di-ver-tir   al

tra-en sus ti - je-re- ti-llas   pa-ra di-ver-tir   al

tra-en sus ti - je-re-ti-llas   pa-ra di-ver-tir   al

Arioso

⑮

Estribillo a 8

Can-te-mos a- le-gres gus-to-sas y u-ni-das

Can-te-mos a- le-gres gus-to-sas y u-ni-das

Can-te-mos a- le-gres gus-to-sas y u-ni-das

Can-te-mos a- le-gres gus-to-sas y u-ni-das

Can-te-mos a- le-gres gus-to-sas y u-ni-das

Can-te-mos a- le-gres gus-to-sas y u-ni-das

Can-te-mos a- le-gres gus-to-sas y u-ni-das

Can-te-mos a- le-gres gus-to-sas y u-ni-das

tasto solo

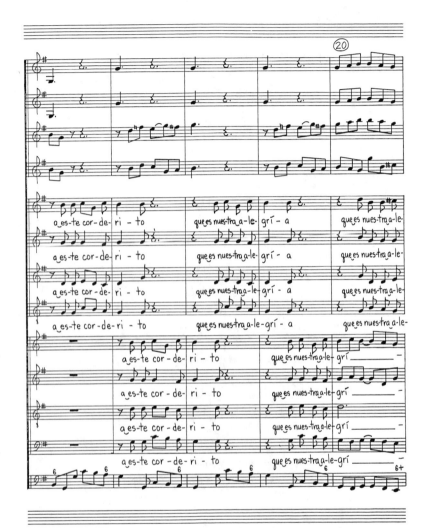

la can-ción gus-to-sa de nues-tra_in-ven-ti _____ - va

la can-ción gus-to-sa de nues-tra_in-ven-ti _____ - va

la can-ción gus-to-sa de nues-tra_in-ven-ti _____ - va

la can-ción gus-to-sa de nues-tra_in-ven-ti _____ - va

la can-ción gus-to-sa de nues-tra_in-ven-ti _____ - va

la can-ción gus-to-sa de nues-tra_in-ven-ti _____ - va

la can-ción gus-to-sa de nues-tra_in-ven-ti _____ - va

la can-ción gus-to-sa de nues-tra_in-ven-ti _____ - va

la can-ción gus-to-sa de nues-tra jn-ven-ti _____ - va

240

241

Algo Andante ㊻

Tonadilla y Coplas a 4
solo

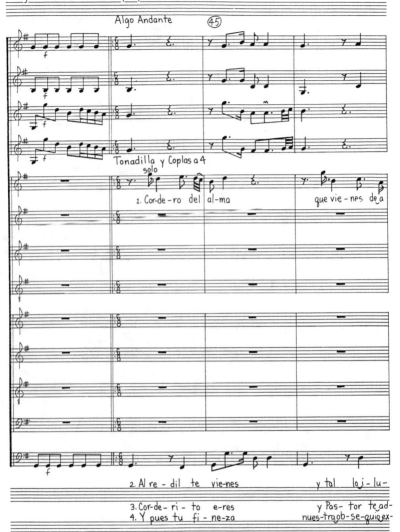

1. Cor-de-ro del al-ma   que vie-nes de a

2. Al re - dil te vie-nes   y tal lo j - lu-
3. Cor-de - ri - to e-res   y Pas- tor te ad-
4. Y pues tu fi - ne-za   nues-tra ob-se-quia ex-

242

rri- ba   a sa – cri- fi-│car-te   por dar-nos la

2. mi- nas   que sien- do de no-che   pa-re- ce que es

3. mi-ran   los que te co- no-cen   fie-les o - ve-

4. ci- ta   hu- mil- de las gra-cias   te da- mos ren-

vi - da   a sa - cri - fi - car - te por dar-nos la vi - da por dar-nos la

2. dí - a   que sien - do de no-che pa-re-ce que es dí-a pa-re-ce que es

3. ji - tas   los que te co-no-cen fie-les o- ve- ji-tas fie-les o-ve-
4. di - das   hu-mil - de las gra-cias te da-mos ren-di-das te da-mos ren-

244

2. dí-a

3. ji-tas
4. di-das

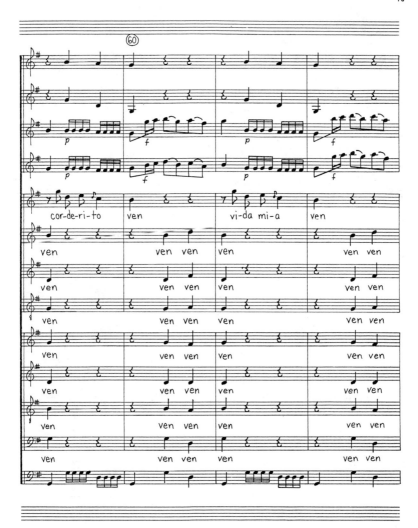

ti-llas con el chas chas chas chas chas chas chas chas chas chas chas chas chas chas de la pri-

ti-llas   chas   chas   chas   chas   de la pri-

ti-llas   chas   chas   chas   chas   de la pri-

ti-llas   chas   chas   chas   chas   de la pri-

ti-llas   chas   chas   chas   chas   de la pri-

ti-llas   chas   chas   chas   chas   de la pri-

ti-llas   chas   chas   chas   chas   de la pri-

ti-llas   chas   chas   chas   chas   de la pri-

sa   con el chas chas chas chas chas chas chas chas chas chas chas chas chas chas   de la pri-

sa   chas   chas   chas   de la pri-

sa   chas   chas   chas   de la pri-

sa   chas   chas   chas   de la pri-

sa   chas   chas   chas   de la pri-

sa   chas   chas   chas   de la pri-

sa   chas   chas   chas   de la pri-

sa   chas   chas   chas   de la pri-

sa de la pri - sa
sa de la pri - sa
sa de la pri - sa
sa de la pri - sa
sa de la pri - sa
sa de la pri - sa
sa de la pri - sa
sa de la pri - sa

254

Villancicos de Kalenda

al Santísimo con

Violines, Oboes, Trompas y Clarines

"Alados Celestiales"

Año 1754

Villancico de Kalenda al Santísimo — Maestro Iribarren Año 1754

Entrada Arioso

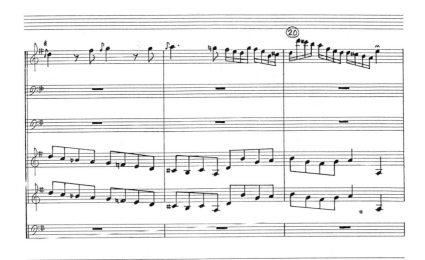

A-la-dos ce-les-tia-les que-ru-bi-nes

a-cla-mad   por el or-be y suscon-fi-nes

tasto solo

la fi-ne-za ma-yor de he-roi-co a-nhe-lo

pues la tie-rra se a-
pues la tie-rra se a-
pues la tie-rra se a-
pues la tie-rra se a-
pues la tie-rra se a-
pues la tie-rra se a-
pues la tie-rra se a-

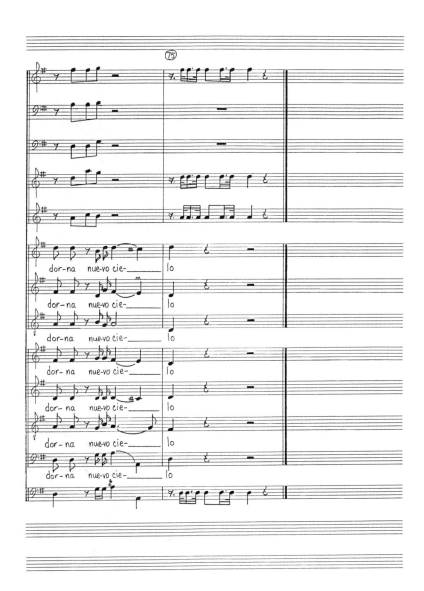

dor-na   nue-vo cie-_____ lo

dor-na   nue-vo cie-_____ lo

dor-na   nue-vo cie-_____ lo

dor-na   nue-vo cie-_____ lo

dor-na   nue-vo cie-_____ lo

dor-na   nue-vo cie-_____ lo

dor-na   nue-vo cie-_____ lo

Aria Arioso a 7 y Solo

273

tad   can-tad so-bre las   nu-bes   can-tad en dul-ces   co-_____

tad   can-tad

tad   can-tad

tad   can-tad

tad   can-tad

tad   can-tad

tad   can-tad

[co]-_____ ros   can-tad   fi-_ ne-___za___

can-tad   can-tad can-tad

can-tad   can-tad can-tad

can-tad   can-tad

can-tad   can-tad

can-tad   can-tad

can- tad   can-tad

281

can-tad

no-_____ ros   can-tad en dul-ces   co-_____ ros

can-tad

no-_____ ros   can-tad en dul-ces   co-_____ ros

can-|tad

can-|tad

can-|tad

can-|tad   can-

can-tad   can-

fi - ne-_____ za la ma- yor _____ _____

can-tad

can-tad

nu-bes

nu-bes

bes

bes

[no-]_____ ros fi-ne-za la ma-__ yor fi-ne-za la ma-

fi-ne-za la ma-

fi-ne-za la ma-

tad · · · · · · · fi-ne-za la ma-

tad · · · · · · · fi-ne-za la ma-

tad · · · · · · · fi-ne-za la ma-

tad · · · · · · · fi-ne-za la ma-

287

288

tad fie-les que-ru-_____ bes a- le-gres y so- no-_____

can-tad

can-tad

can-tad

can-tad

can-tad

can-tad

ros can-tad   can-tad   can-tad so-bre las nu—

can-tad   can-tad

can-tad   can- tad

can-tad   can-tad can- tad

can-tad   can-tad can- tad

can-tad   can-tad can- tad

can-tad   can-tad can- tad

bes   can-|tad en dul-ces | co-_____ | ros   fi - | ne-___za

can-tad   can-tad

can-tad   can-tad

can-tad   can-tad

can-tad   can-tad

can-tad   can-tad

can-tad   can-tad

la ma- yor fi- ne____ ____ za la ma- yor   can-tad

a- le- gres y so- no-ros

a- le- gres y so- no-ros

can-

can-

can-

can-

co-_____ ros   a- le-___ gres y   so- no-_____

can-tad

can-tad

can-tad

can-tad

can-tad

can-tad

ros   can-tad fie-les que- ru-_____ bes fi- ne-___ __ za la ma-

can-tad   fi- ne-za la ma-

can-tad   fi- ne-za la ma-

can-tad   fi- ne-za la ma-

can-tad   fi- ne-za la ma-

can-tad   fi- ne-za la ma-

302

303

tier-no Dios de a-mo————res   can-tad le con pri- mo————

305

307

glo-_____ ria   nos brin- da con   su a mo-_____

[mo-] _____ _____ _____ r   nos brin-da

nos brin-da

nos brin-da

nos brin-da

nos brin-da

nos brin-da

nos brin-da

Villancico de Kalenda de Corpus a 8

con Violines y Oboes

"Las Aves Acordes"

Año 1756

Villancico de Kalenda de Corpus a 8   Maestro Iribarren Año 1756

Entrada, Allegro Gustoso

313

314

Las

Las

ros los vien——tos

vien——tos

vien——tos

ros los vien——tos

a Duo

en dul——ces ca-den-

en dul——ces ca-den-

317

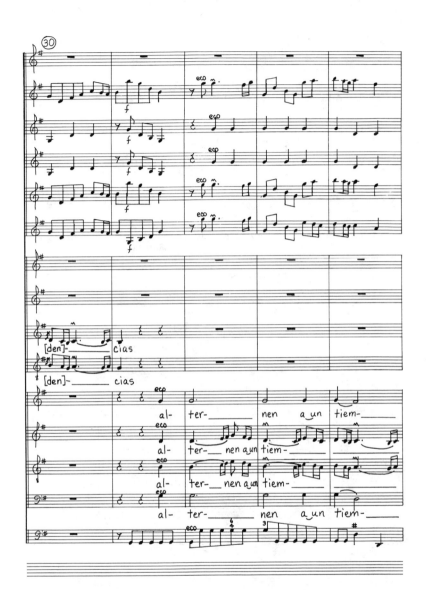

318

319

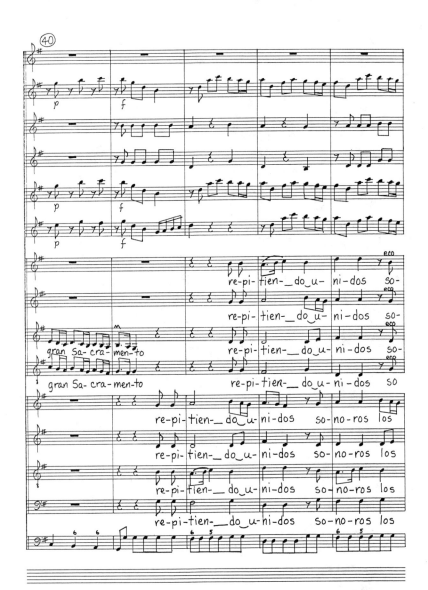

gran Sa-cra-men-to
re-pi-tien-_do_u-ni-dos so-
re-pi-tien-_do_u-ni-dos so-
gran Sa-cra-men-to   re-pi-tien-_do_u-ni-dos so-
gran Sa-cra-men-to   re-pi-tien-_do_u-ni-dos so
re-pi-tien-_do_u-ni-dos so-no-ros los
re-pi-tien-_do_u-ni-dos so-no-ros los
re-pi-tien-_do_u-ni-dos so-no-ros los
re-pi-tien-_do_u-ni-dos so-no-ros los

321

Que duer-me mi a

ce

322

des-can-sa mi vi-_____ da   ce

des-can-sa mi vi-da   ce

des-can-sa mi vi-da   ce

des-can-sa mi vi-_____ da

ce   ce

ce   ce

ce   ce

ce   ce

des-can-_____ _____ sa mi cie-_____ lo

des-can-_____ _____ sa mi cie-_____ lo

des-can-_____ _____ sa mi cie-_____ lo

des-can-_____ _____ sa mi cie-_____ lo

des-can-_____ _____ sa mi cie-_____ lo

des-can-_____ _____ sa mi cie-_____ lo

des-can-_____ _____ sa mi cie-_____ lo

des-can-_____ _____ sa mi cie-_____ lo

326

Recitativo

Tiple 2°
1° Coro

En e-sa a-zul cam-pa-ña di-la-ta-da

Alto
1° Coro

los plu-

Acompañamiento

de tan-to bien la glo-ria du-pli-ca-da

ma-dos va-je-les ma-ti-za-dos ce-

a Duo

por que re-sue-ne al vien-to la gra-cia sin-gu-

le-bren con a-cen-tos a-cor-da-dos por que re-sue-ne al vien-to la gra-cia sin-gu-

lar del Sa-cra- men- to

lar del Sa-cra- men- to

327

331

tor-___to-la su-a- ve

la a-man-___te Fi-___lo-me-na

332

tri-___ ne so-no-ra y gra- ve

can-___ te sin sus-to y pe- na

a Duo

al

al

mas di-vi-no Pa-

mas di-vi-no Pa-

tri-_ne so-no-toy gra-_ve sin sus-toy pe-_na al mas di-vi-no Pa-_

can-_te sin sus-toy pe-_na al mas di-vi-no Pa-_

335

al mas di-vi- no Pa_____

[Pa-]_____ n

[Pa-]_____ al mas di-vi- no Pa-

_n al mas di-vi- no   Pan

_n al mas di-vi- no   Pan

La tor-___to-la su-a-ve

la-a-man-___te

tri- ne so-no-ray gra- ve

al mos di-vi-no

fi- lo-me-na

can-—te sin sus-toy pe- na

al mos di-vi-no

tri-_____ne

[al] mas di-vi-no Pa-_____

can-_____te

al mas di-vi- no Pa-_____

_n al mas di-vi — no   Pan

_n al mas di-vi — no   Pan

tasto solo

345

Por que al mi-rar an-sio-sa

Res-

el al-ma tan-ta a-mor

347

pi-ra ya go-zo-——sa   solo   con don tan

y-a-lien-ta su te-mor   su te-mor   condon tan

tasto solo

[D.C. al fine]

ce—les—tial   con don tan ce-les-tial____ tan   ce—les—tial

ce—les—tial   con don tan ce-les-tial____ tan   ce—les—tial

349

DATE DUE
